The Treasure: Healing the Hurt of the Post Modern Heart

The Treasure: Healing the Hurt of the Post Modern Heart

Dr. Glen B. Maiden

To order additional copies of this book, contact:
Xlibris Corporation
1-888-795-4274
www.Xlibris.com
Orders@Xlibris.com
95401

Contents

Acknowledgements 7

Prologue 9

Introduction: The Treasure 15

SECTION ONE: POST MODERN PAIN

Addictions "R" Us Community Church 33

Healing Survivors of Trauma 46

Perfect People Syndrome 58

SECTION TWO: THE BIBLICAL STORY OF HEALING LIFE'S HURTS

Attachment, Addiction, and Idolatry 67

The Power of Brokenness 82

Prayer Heals the Heart 99

Heroes 133

SECTION THREE: A REVOLUTION OF HEALING THE HEART

Growing Deeper 143

GOD DNA 151

Belonging 160

REAL Community 170

The Treasure of My Heart . . . The Bride 183

Conclusion 195

Bibliography 203

Acknowledgements

I WOULD LIKE to thank my lovely wife and children for their support to serve Jesus in the 'hood. We lived in poverty for years to launch the inner city church. Lori and kids endured my sleepless nights and compulsive phone calls as I managed a community of hurt people. During this challenging time Lori, kids, and I lived with her mother, Loretta. Her support through the lean years in the 'hood made a huge impact. My amazing family did all this without complaint. Thank you Lori, Melanie, Daniel, and Emily. You are my greatest work.

I also thank my inner city staff for their devotion for over a decade of hard work on one of the most dangerous street corners in America. Kim F., Bob A., Aaron and Gail B., Beth B., Los and Sarah A., Sue K., I am humbled by your devotion. For the staff which helped launched the work into the suburbs and continued the work for hurt people, Gerri G., Chip H., Lori A., Davine C., Beth H.; thank you. Your dedication is stunning. For Tracy H. and Lynn M. who helped transcribe and edit, you are treasure.

I also want to give my appreciation to several friends who share their stories in *The Treasure*. You are my heroes. Many thanks to Julie Nelson, an amazing and aspiring photographer who provided the awesome cover. You can check out her work at julieannelson.com. Thanks Julie. Go Ducks.

Finally, I wish to thank my mother, Eula Mae. She always believed, persevered, prayed, loved, treated kindly, and supported the vision of reaching people. Thanks Mom.

Prologue

EXQUISITE COASTAL PANORA-
mas emerge when winter squalls
surrender cold rage. Blue sky emancipates storm weary souls as rain clouds break
up and light breaches out.

This same beautiful transformation emerges for the human heart. When healing
happens, grace tenderly touches gale force guilt. Hope like tears swells rich. Serial
emptiness erupts into wholeness, blended families rebuild, singleness grows, addict
personalities repair, and survivors mend.

The Treasure tells the true story of healing and hope in my inner-city ministry
on the west coast of Michigan. My experience there helped me to witness firsthand
how a transformational intimate community brings wholeness to the hurt of post
modern friends and family suffering from addiction and trauma. Serving and surviving
as a pastor in the inner city also enabled me to comprehend that all communities to
a greater or lesser degree face the challenges of addiction and trauma. Finally, my
time in the 'hood inspired an alternative model for church growth. I have a deep
commitment to spiritual growth and have traveled from seminar to mini camp
seeking models to implement. I sensed a poor fit with my story of ministry, and I
come to the realization that I did not need to journey far, one unearthed right under
my nose as the attendees of my church and I grappled with being the presence of
Christ in one of the most violent drug-filled neighborhoods in Michigan. My book
divides into three sections: Post Modern Pain; The Biblical Story of Healing Life's
Hurts; and A Revolution of Healing the Heart.

Section one describes the addiction and victimization in our coastal community.
I uncover groundbreaking work in the catalyst of addiction called, anxiety reaction.

This piece discusses in layman terms the neurological nature of addiction, the anatomy of trauma, and the power of God's grace to touch both.

Section two, The Biblical Story of Healing Life's Hurts, connects the process of overcoming addiction with God's grace. In this portion I show how addiction follows the same progression as idolatry. Brokenness begins the transformational journey. The bottom of life opens the doorway for God's grace and power. In this section I tell a personal story of discovering my own trauma.

Section three, A Revolution of Healing the Heart, casts a vision for the healing of idolatry, addiction, and trauma as the foundation of the missional church movement. Historically church growth specialists tend to focus on numbers, programs, bullet point strategy statements and facilities. Emergent church analysts speak of the post modern experience, but do not address the nuts and bolts of intensely personal issues of addiction and trauma. *The Treasure* demonstrates the transformational presence of Christ within transparent small group communities of Christians as the growth edge.

I served the inner city church plant in Michigan for 17 years. Part of the reason for the lengthy tenure is that I engaged people with multiple theological traditions by avoiding denominational politics and emphasizing the atoning work of Christ. This Christology forms the unifying principle in a church community of varied backgrounds; Reformed, Wesleyan, Catholic, Charismatic and others. I operated with a comfort level serving such a church because my own religious background is so inter-denominational.

My formative religious training began in a mainline liturgical denomination. My college experience was Wesleyan with a view toward spontaneous spiritual revival. The preaching focused on experiencing purity of life and love through a second event of sanctification. The message rotated around sin/redemption, humanity is broken and in need of immediate salvific cure.

The first church in which I served was inter-racial, inter-denominational, hyper–choice, and emphasized flawless behavior as the means to purity of life. Sin/redemption/ judgment framed the message. This means that a human is not only broken by sin, in need of immediate redemption, but God's judgment looms in the offing. The criterion for blessing or judgment was the perfect behavior of the congregants. The 2-3 hour church services were on the one hand grace filled and emotional, and on the other profoundly judgmental. Drawn in close to the presence of God, one then felt slapped into submission. One attendee commented after a particularly pointed sermon, "I feel as though I was dragged naked across a field of sharp stones." The press for immediate repentance and decision was strong. As I now look back on this experience, I retain a picture of God as a grace-intoxicated, borderline personality suffering from high-anxiety over human imperfection.

My seminary training was Calvinistic. The concept of election refreshed, as you can imagine, when set against the backdrop of a "grace-intoxicated, borderline personality God." I had a sense that I had come home. There I experienced a deep respect for Scripture. This too was stunning to me because I did not expect this from a mainline denomination. My professors introduced me to the works of John Calvin and Jonathan Edwards. The depth of God's sovereignty, control, presence and the high regard for Scripture still inspire me. I have seen many opportunities in ministry to combine these with the best of the Wesleyan tradition.

The church whose history I record launched on a mega-church model. This system originated from a Reformed background in process evangelism, the use of contemporary music and arts, intense discipleship through small groups, and a creation theology. Creation theology focuses on redemption as grace driven process. God is at work in presence, in power, in personality moving the entire created order to redemption. The church is comprised mostly of addicts and survivors of trauma. Consistent counseling, support, follow up make up the means of growth and survival. Not only do we address addiction and trauma at the personal level, but we create a counter culture of intimate community standing against the family and social systems undermining the addict and victim.

Our constituents are of many different backgrounds and theologies. To harmonize this group toward common goals, I avoid theological slogans and hot button hierarchical issues. I focus strongly on the work of Christ in atoning for the sins of the world, and the work of the Spirit in forming a biblical community through the intimacy of small groups. As Christ in the Spirit binds people together with Him, the intimacy that one experiences is the source of joy in life and the assurance of one's salvation. In our church context, I teach that all people seek this intimacy and that addictions are misguided attempts to find it—a version of Augustine's, our hearts are restless until they find their rest in God. This helps addicts to see how their behaviors have spiritual significance and to see how they can be accepted and loved by God.

Some might find my theology eclectic and perhaps inconsistent. But my experience is that I have learned from the different traditions that have been part of my life I have been able to blend them together into a theology that has been meaningful to me and to my community. I believe God loves and has appropriate control. He decrees sovereignly. He calls and chooses whom He loves. This love is the motivational foundation of all He does in creation and redemption. Love requires choice. Grace is God's gift, and He invites humans to receive it. In my theology God calls, He chooses, and He wraps His arms around those who embrace Him in return. God works in process. He guides through providence. He creates at all times. There is profound presence of God performing in each breath, each drink, each meal, and each contact with neighbors. God is near and we belong to Him.

God does not need us, He wants us. In this economy of love, response is reasonable. The action of the beloved is not the criterion for salvation, but without embrace grace cannot be known and experienced. Working with addicts and survivors is a practical example. A choice must be made to heal. God provides His riches of recovery, but they cannot be tasted without a step toward relationship.

I also have witnessed that recovery is a wonder of God's unrelenting creative presence. He sustains, He forgives, and He carries. Therefore, I consider myself an inter-denominational denominationalist with deep Calvinistic roots expressed in Wesley-like passion for renewal.

The stories I tell are graphic, not the norm for the average suburban church but touch the core of experiences Christians tend to fog over. From bikers to Baptists, Methodists to methamphetamine addicts, charismatics to crack heads, and Presbyterians to post modern porn addicts, the most addicted–traumatized people I have ever known experienced wholeness and help. I am convinced that these stories relate to readers. The accounts have power not only because they are true, but because they bring readers to a panoramic point about their own trauma. Due to the extreme nature of human tragedy, I have changed names, genders, and details. In fact I have purposely kept the name of the church anonymous to protect her identity. Every description of addiction and trauma has been altered to protect identities. None of the stories are fictitious.

Any believing person, missional community, or traditional denomination can experience wholeness for addiction and trauma within transformational intimate community. This is the storyline of the project.

The subject of my book brings to light the treasure of God's love for people in a roller coaster cultural revolution called post modernism. This new era does not assume foundational Christian truth. The uncertainty of economic change, distrust for authority and church traditions, broken families, and the need to belong to a deeper spirituality highlight the ideology. In this context God seeks to touch the deepest hurt of the human heart. He does this through the work of Christ's spirit in transformational small groups of Christians, not Sunday school, but deep intimate relationships of love and care. When an entire Christian community focuses on healing, phenomena happen. Real life horror stories find grace and mercy. Lives change, the unacceptable find belonging, and the broken discover wholeness. Survivors of unimaginable trauma clothed in shame drink in the wonder of God's presence in community.

Healing also happens in proximity to God's word, the Bible. Woven throughout *The Treasure* is Scripture. I have a loving devotion to the speech of God and desire with all my heart to be true to the rhythms of His Spirit and word. This book examines a never seen before treatment of the treasure passages of the Old and New Testaments exploring their context and relevance for healing trauma in a post modern culture.

Church growth authors focus on programs, numbers, bullet point purpose statements, strategies for multiplication, and philosophical analysis. I think these approaches can be helpful, but can also lead to tragedy. To reduce God's heart to lists and theoretical systems becomes ministry malpractice. Mega church growth movements can foster denial. Consumerist mentalities trigger deeper addictions to success; numbers, tools for ministry, equipment, and production. Post modern analysis without the experience of transformation has the potential to create reactionaries rather than revolutionaries. God's word within intimate community gently unearths a treasure for healing people. This vision costs nothing but surrender to the riches of Christ, and the truth about us.

A beautiful transformation happens in a small group of caring Christians. Acceptance, the warmth of belonging, the power of the Spirit all touch the most intimate hurts. Healing begins with an honest moment. A hurt person transparently shares internal trauma, and life change begins. He makes amends, she forgives perpetrators. The grip of searing inner pain releases. Insatiable dogs of addiction rest their fury. The missional church of Jesus Christ as expressed in small groups of believers powerfully heals.

The inner city church I served on the west coast of Michigan became a miracle of grace starting with 9 people, 350 bucks, and a fist full of human tragedy. God tenderly embraced this group of religious refugees comprised mostly of post modern addicts and survivors to become one of the largest and fastest growing churches on the storm tossed coast of Western Michigan.

Finally, *The Treasure* possesses some unique features. I believe you will find the catalyst of addiction and trauma, anxiety reaction, and the power of the Spirit in biblical community to open the door for amazing healing in your life. The study of the treasure passages has never been seen before. *The Treasure* stands on groundbreaking work. You can use this book as a Bible study to teach people how to reach out, heal, and grow. You will find exposition of the biblical text and questions for your group after each chapter. Finally, *The Treasure* will teach you how to write and rewrite your own story. After each chapter I will walk you through the telling of your spiritual journey and introduce you to some friends of mine to help you. In the end you will be able to see God's hand in your life and watch as treasure emerges in your story.

I hope you will share the gift of your story with many people. In fact I will donate proceeds from *The Treasure* to a scholarship fund for people to enter recovery. You may reach me at *dr.glenmaiden@gmail.com* or www.glenmaiden.com. Give me a profile of a friend or family member who needs recovery and we will do our best to offer financial support. I found this inspiration in a post modern shoe manufacturer who with each purchase donates a pair of shoes to underprivileged children. What if we create a Tsunami of support for the global millions suffering from addiction and trauma? Perhaps your faith community would like to use *The Treasure* as a teaching base and at the same time finance people in your community to receive support. Let me know how we can help. Now friends, let the revolution begin!

Introduction

The Treasure

PICTURES OF GOD in the Scriptures proliferate: He is shield, refuge; Jesus is light, door, good shepherd . . . the list goes on. One powerful image in the Scriptures, one that does not get much attention, but one that has become transformational to the church I planted is this: God is a treasure. In my experience, the image of God in Jesus as a treasure has been a potent influence in helping post modern people to overcome life's hurt.

Like all imagery in Scripture, "treasure" has deep spiritual meaning. In both the Old ('otsar) and New (thesaurus) Testaments the picture connects to the world of kings and queens. It refers to the gold and silver that royalty gather in the "treasury". These precious metals formed the currency in the ancient world and had value beyond any of the other stuff of life because of rarity and beauty. With gold and silver one possessed power to buy necessities, whether clothing, food, or building material. A full treasury proclaimed royal strength. Some of the gold and silver they gathered through conquest; some of it they received as gifts from other nations. The treasury solidified dynastic potency and permanence. All nations go through good times and bad, and a full treasury stabilized a nation during anxious circumstances (Thomas A. Boogaart, Lecture on Biblical Images).

There is a long tradition in Scripture of taking this treasure image and applying it to God in Christ. The image applies in a number of different but inter related ways. Initially, God who in His being, wisdom, love, and intimate knowing is a treasure. It relates next to the gifts that come from God to those who live in relationship with Him. God calls His law a treasure; God characterizes listening and loving His people as treasure; God's power poured into "clay jars" of human weakness unearths as a treasure. Finally treasure touches the people whom God has chosen to be in relationship to Him. God calls the people of Israel His treasure as well as His kingdom community in the famous parable. They possess value, power, and transformation because God's favor embraces them; they store within themselves the riches God wants to give to the world. If we look at all these different uses of treasure in Scripture, we see they connect. Treasure emerges as life-giving power. It begins in God, proceeds from God, and transforms everything it touches (Thomas A. Boogaart, Lecture on Biblical Images).

Teaching these treasure passages to my friends as they heal has made me sensitive to still other nuances of meaning in the Bible. Treasure as life-giving force and transformation opposes what the world understands to be power. One counter cultural nuance suggests that God gives strength to the weak and broken, His treasure. God set His heart on the people of Israel not because she was the greatest of the nations, but because of her weakness: *"It is not because you were more numerous than any of the other people that the Lord set His heart on you and chose you-for you were the fewest of all peoples" (Deuteronomy 7.7)*. Again: *"Do not say my power and might of my own hand got me this wealth. But remember the Lord your God, for it is He who gives you power to get wealth . . . . " (Deuteronomy 8.17-18)*. As Paul says, *"We have this treasure in clay jars so that it may be clear that this extraordinary power belongs to God and does not come from us" (2 Corinthians 4.7 NIV)*. A second shade uncovers a hidden quality. God's treasure reveals in places where the rest of the world does not look, often among the broken and outcast. A third fine distinction uncovers anxiety as the root problem for people who set their hearts on false treasure. Jesus makes this explicit in the Sermon on the Mount with His call, *"Do not be anxious . . . . "* As I describe below, Scripture makes a strong connection between addiction and anxiety, and we in our congregation deal with this all the time. Because of this, the treasure passages speak powerfully. I will review some of these passages and their role in the healing of addicts and survivors in a post modern church setting.

> *The Kingdom of heaven is like treasure hidden in a field. When a man found it, he hid it again, and then in his joy went and sold all he had and bought that field. Again, the kingdom of heaven is like a merchant looking for fine pearls. When he found one of great value, he went away and sold everything he had and bought it. Matthew 13:44 NIV*

This treasure passage appears in the Gospel of Matthew teaching section of parables about God's intimate kingdom community. The first parable mentions the sower and the seed. Jesus illustrates the people who hear God's word with various levels of understanding and response. Christ characterizes followers who listen and understand the message as deeply devout. The second parable illustrates the weeds. Enter divine judgment. Jesus states that transformed followers will face double-agents, advocates of the enemy undermining spiritual solidarity. Jesus calls for awareness and patience until the Day of Judgment at which time the covert moles will be culled from real community. The mustard seed and the yeast form the third and fourth parables. Jesus contrasts the good seed which defines authentic kingdom community with the weeds, the chaotic components causing imbalance. The fifth parable cites the treasure passage referred to in my work. The sixth parable, the pearl, appears as a thematic repetition of the treasure. Intimate Christian community has inherent value, it delights, and individuals experience its depth through surrender and loving loyalty. The seventh and final parable is the net. This story again looks forward to a time of judgment when double-agents will suffer separation as opposed to God's kingdom community gathered for grace.

The piece ends with another treasure passage. Jesus encourages teachers of the law saying, *"Therefore every teacher of the law who has been instructed about the kingdom of heaven is like the owner of a house who brings out of his storeroom new treasures as well as old" Matthew 13.52 NIV.* Jesus infers that a teacher of the law who understands His message not only experiences wealth in the wonder of God's heart laws, but finds fresh power within a transforming community.

In Matthew 13.44 Jesus spoke of the kingdom as a treasure. He saw a deeper, under-the-radar value in God's rule and presence among His people. This component to healing community possesses undercover power. The treasure of intimate kingdom community though vague, at the same time reveals deep spirituality.

This parable parallels the story of our missional church plant in an inner city war zone of automatic weapons fire, bullet holes, beatings, and burglaries. In the late 80's, nine young Christian friends with 350 bucks launched a church in the center of one of the most dangerous, drug-trafficking districts of Western Michigan. Armed with a contemporary church growth plan loaded with bullet point purpose statements we set out to change the world. But on a violent street among run-down homes and broken lives we unearthed a richer, deeper spiritual journey gripping the heart with grace. Jesus talked about it minus strategies. He called it treasure, obscure, under-the-radar, and life transforming.

Our urban church building stands at the corner of Terrace and Irwin. This building in the 'hood claims famous history. Jim Bakker, the fallen, now restored evangelist from the 80's, attended church in our location as a youth.

The place assaulted the senses. The blue stained façade accented the Barney purple cinder blocks on either side. Red carpet spread everywhere. The building looked more like a bordello than a place of worship. The smell was offensive. Having stood for 50 years, it not only had the odor of a broom closet filled with old wet mops, parts of it had a dank, prison like quality. In fact, we affectionately called our children's department the dungeon. In winter we also called it the meat locker due to the cold. The restrooms were horrid, often overflowing from clogged sewer pipes. Our regular attendees felt it their moral duty to warn visiting friends to "go" before they visited our church services. The men's room had a flusher on the urinal hurling water upward and outward when one pulled the handle. The regulars learned to flush, zip, hop, bob and weave all at the same time. Our building gave sensitive folk nightmares. Shot at, bled upon, burglars broke in and sacked it numerous times. In retrospect, it was the worst environment imaginable to plant a church.

We warmly called our neighborhood The Knife and Gun Club because of the beatings, bullet holes, and burglaries. One Sunday morning after service a drug bust across the street greeted our worshipers complete with squad cars and strobe lights. On the opposite corner of Terrace and Irwin a printer of porn operated a "900" sex hotline. I spoke with the owner of the sex store. He expressed concern for his staff that, in turn, feared to work in the location due to drive-by shootings with bullets blasting down the hallway. During a board meeting one evening we looked out the window and witnessed our county prosecutor amassing his SWAT team in our parking lot. They finalized their strategy, put on black windbreakers with large yellow letters – POLICE, strapped on side arms over blue jeans, then locked and loaded their shotguns. I remember because one of our deacons showed up late just as the police unpacked their arsenal of weapons. I remarked as the deacon came in to the meeting, "Our prosecutor wants to discuss your tardiness to board meetings." I love teachable moments. And then, the Terrace Street Streaker. While rehearsing before Sunday's service, our musicians witnessed a woman sprinting down the street clad only in her birthday suit. The streaker pursued her boyfriend as fast as her bare feet would bear her. The reason our streaker did the chasing and not the fleeing . . . the butcher knife in her hand.

Finally . . . our town. Seventy-two percent divorce rate. Alcoholism and drugs rampant. Automobile-dependent factory closings, victims of the downsizing of the car industry. Double-digit unemployment. Our city claims fame for being the capitol of two dubious categories: sexually transmitted diseases and beer tents (Editor, 2002).

Make a list of the most awful places on the planet to start a church. From facility to neighborhood to dying community, we found ourselves in the most growth-prohibiting location imaginable. Fortunately, God doesn't live by lists and bullet point strategies. His heart beats a different rhythm. In this violent locale, addicts and survivors found wholeness and help. Scores of traumatized people experienced life transformation through Christ. Wholeness replaced brokenness. In the most terrible spot in this hemisphere to plant a church we found the deeper, the richer. Jesus said it: A treasure in life emerges in unexpected places – worthy of sacrifice. This transformational richness uncovers in surrender and serenity follows.

At the Tucson Gem and Mineral show, a rock hound found a blue violet stone the size of a potato. It cost 15 dollars. Not as pretty as the others, the vendor offered

10 bucks. The rock connoisseur cleaned, buffed and then certified it as a 1905 carat natural star sapphire–800 carats larger than the biggest stone of its kind. The value? 2.28 million dollars. It took a man passionate about stones to look beyond the grime and recognize the treasure within. Jesus talks about this. Treasure transforms (Smith, 2001).

God Almighty will be your treasure, more wealth than you can imagine.
You'll take delight in God, the Mighty one, and look to Him joyfully, boldly.
You'll pray to Him and He'll listen; He'll help you do what you've promised.
Job 22:25 MSG

The second treasure passage comes from Eliphaz, one of Job's alleged comforters. Eliphaz exhorts Job to *"submit . . . lay up His words in your heart . . . return to the Almighty" Job 22.21-26 NIV.* Then, after the submitting, laying up, and returning, God will once again be Job's treasure. Eliphaz counsels Job about life on the other side of trauma. After this process of surrender, he compares relationship with God to treasure, wealth. Inner joy and delight describe the emotions Job will feel in this relationship. God's personal attention will accent Job's prayer life. Job's friends have wisdom; they inherit great tradition, but they use it inappropriately in their counsel. God says at the end of the book that they did not speak what is right. Even though Eliphaz miscalculated the diagnosis of Job's tragedy, his words resonate. Deeper relationship with God can be experienced through suffering. This depth has special meaning for post modern addicts and survivors who seek healing.

Job's brokenness, overcoming adversity, and experiencing God through trauma parallels our inner city story beautifully. The chronicle of post modern addicts and survivors finding strength in their weakness, and experiencing belonging with a God who values them chronicles Job's life. God is our treasure in which we delight. The richness emerges because God listens, he engages. This listening results in helping.

It's hard to hear when you fear for your life. Our building was horrible. The violent neighborhood drove the timid seeker away. We emerged a community of faith broken by life wrapping our arms around the One who pays attention and helps. In this terrible locale, God answered prayer and His faithfulness found us. God listened in unspeakable places and changed lives. Listening is a transformational treasure.

I have a confession to make. I don't listen well. I call it "selective hearing disorder." I hear what I want to hear, to my detriment. I have three beautiful children–Melanie, Dan, and Emily. They are the delight of my life. Want to make me cry? Let's talk about my kids. I love my wife, Lori. After many years of marriage I still chase her until she lets me catch her. With deep love and commitment to my wife and children . . . I left them at church . . . in the violent 'hood . . . alone. The crime occurred after a Sunday morning service. We normally traveled in two vehicles but this day we drove one. I spoke with Lori at the front of the Barney purple building and she asked me to pick up the children and her on the concrete steps. En route to our blue mini-van I met someone . . . a brief counseling moment . . . distraction. I will never forget the anxiety as I drove into my garage, and then panic . . . I left my family on the front steps of the church building in a war zone! I broke laws as I raced back to get them. Then it happened . . . rain.

I failed to listen and I abandoned my treasures in the inner city with porn shops, automatic weapons, and now, cold bone chilling rain. Turning the corner into the 'hood I found them alive walking home in the downpour. I ushered them into the car apologizing, groveling, and pleading for forgiveness. Lori was kind, tenderhearted, and compassionate. Clearly she understood my stress, being susceptible to listening disorders. I started to feel better. My young soggy son, Dan, sat in the back seat. In his sweet, prepubescent voice he said, "Daddy." "Yes son." "Daddy, Mommy thinks you're stupid." I shook my head in total agreement. If stupid is not listening . . . then I have this thing. God listens. He does not abandon, betray, forget. Listening defines the deeper way.

> *My goal is that they may be encouraged in heart, united in love, so that they*
> *have the full riches of complete understanding in order that they may know*
> *the mystery of God, namely, Christ in whom are hidden all the treasures of*
> *wisdom and knowledge . . . He forgave us all our sins, having cancelled the*
> *charge of our legal indebtedness, which stood against us and condemned us; He*
> *has taken it away, nailing it to the cross.*
> *Colossians 2.2-3; 13-14 NIV*

The third treasure passage comes from Paul's letter to the Colossians. Imprisoned Paul inspires the infant church. He directs her to the *summum bonum* of the spiritual journey. The greatest good unearths not as religious regulations, nor human traditions, but Christ. The context of this passage is critical. The Apostle incarcerated faces martyrdom. Paul possesses a spiritual component deep within transcending his confinement. This relationship with God has the capacity and character to touch and inspire the internal captivity of the embryonic church tenderly pointing her to the treasure of Paul's heart, Christ. Though jailed, Paul thinks and feels something deeper than his circumstances liberating anxiety with courage, unity, and fullness of relationship with God.

Follow the historical record. A think tank from the East discovered Christ in a contaminated corral for third world livestock. Jesus labored sweating in a blue-collar workshop in the armpit of Israel. Horrible locations, unsanitary conditions, hurting people, recession, political oppression, hopelessness. One follower said about Jesus' beginnings, *"Can anything good come from Nazareth?" John 1:46 NIV*. The treasure appears in the midst of wrecked humanity and shattered dreams bringing light and love.

In the inner city, with Barney purple paint, bordello red carpet and unsanitary smells, God listens and He helps. Without cathedrals or cash flow, the treasure transpires . . . the soft slap of Galilean sandals bearing a message of grace, a delicate drawl perfected in the gentle hills of Nazareth, preaching peace. He tenderly forgives my sin and shame. Jesus is the treasure. He listens. He cares about wounds and worry. The treasure is beyond imagination . . . the delight, the joy, the courage.

Although purposeful programming and missional theories helped in the 'hood, they possess no power to heal the deepest hurts of wounded worshipers. The richer part of the spiritual journey relates to connection with Christ's spirit in small groups of transforming people holding high the value of community and God's word. He loves addicts and survivors of trauma. Jesus is the hidden treasure, and He treasures the traumatized in their hiddenness. Church growth experts produce lists as though embracing steps or purpose statements can cause a faith community to prevail. The emergent church movement has generated much ideology and reflection, but may lure itself into a paralysis of analysis missing the deeper message of post modern Christianity which is . . . treasure. The treasure reflects the transformational image of God in a spirit filled community of healing Christians. Paul the Apostle states that lists and human traditions cannot be the greatest good—growth strategies and man made analyses included. The treasure uncovers as Christ.

An icy wonderland describes Christmas time in Michigan. Drifting snow banks sparkle like diamonds. Soft flakes of frozen sky gently cover the earth with newness. By February, winter tells a different tale with long nights, winter winds, sunless days. Snow loses its romance and we call it a nuisance, the horrible white stuff, slop. In the 'hood, February forbids and forebodes—barren trees expose worn-out houses, cracked windowpanes, and broken lives-not so wonderful.

One frigid Friday evening our secretary called me at home and said, "Pastor Glen, I hear a man pounding on the front door of the building. He wants me to let him in. He says he will kill himself. Do I let him in?" A lesson in "Pastoring in the 'Hood 101"—do not let armed suicidal-men into the building with the secretary! I called the police and communicated he had a gun (I discovered that if you want quick service from police tell them there is a weapon). When I arrived, several squad cars and an ambulance surrounded the man. He didn't carry a gun. He brandished a knife with which he deeply gashed his wrists then thrashed his fists against the glass double doors of the Barney purple building. Staggering next door he collapsed behind a tree bleeding to death. The ambulance and police convoy left with the man, the secretary went home, and Lori and I stood on the front steps of the building. Blood traced everywhere.

Think about the first ten minutes of *Saving Private Ryan*, or a news clip from Baghdad. It looked like the Passover. Low velocity blood spatter with dark red hand prints painted eerie images on the aluminum doorframe and windows. I had no idea the human body could exchange such volumes of blood and survive. Lori and I filled a bucket with scalding water, armed ourselves with scrub brushes and washed the glass double doors by hand. As we cleaned coagulating blood, the steam billowed a rich aroma, overwhelming and nauseating. We washed and rinsed watching red gobbets of blood slide down concrete steps onto the frozen street.

Blood teaches. It pulses or we perish. On the wrong side of town, at a knoll called skeletal-skull God listened and blood ran. Planks painted red with a woodworker's palm prints, high velocity spatter clotting on a carpenter's cross, the sweet scent of fluid exchange and Jesus Christ brings us near to God. Through the sacrifice of Christ on the cross we belong. Locked out in the chill of sin and shame, He opens the door to God's heart through the shedding of His blood. Jesus is the treasure and He never tires of forgiving and bringing us near.

God put a gem in the 'hood that frozen February. The church secretary who loved literally saved a man's life. We discovered that church growth cannot be buildings, preachers or politics. Spiritual depth unearths not as a post-modern, post-seeker, mega-growth paradigm, nor can it be a micro-church strategy of obsolescence and death. The treasure is Jesus Christ, stronger than death, deeper than the grave. A Tsunami cannot quench the power of this treasure. Walk through the war zone with us.

> *Today God has reaffirmed that you are dearly held treasure just as He*
> *promised a people entrusted with keeping his commandments a people set high*
> *above all other nations that He's made, high in praise, fame, and honor: you're*
> *a people holy to God, your God.*
> *Deuteronomy 26:18 NIV*

The next treasure passage comes from the Old Testament book of Deuteronomy. This citation characterizes the Israeli kingdom community as "dearly held treasure, high in praise, fame, honor, and holiness." God makes quite a statement. I think it redundant to revisit the foibles, failures, and character defects of the Israelite people. The people tended to do it themselves. Psalm 106 chronicles a classic example: "*We have sinned, even as our ancestors did; we have done wrong and acted wickedly. When our ancestors were in Egypt . . . .*" God loves His imperfect people.

Post modern addicts and survivors of trauma live with intense blame and self hatred. Shame drives the addict to use. Self loathing shrouds survivors. The traumatized soul perceives that she caused the assault, buried alive under layers of worthlessness. This treasure passage reveals God's heart of grace and empathy for His broken people. Intimate healing community as God's treasure uncovers a powerful transformative system in a society that victimizes its own. Communicating high value for post modern addicts and survivors creates a counter culture to smoldering shame and self loathing. We found that wholeness for addiction and trauma cannot happen only with words spoken from a pulpit or in a creed, but transformation takes place with belonging and value touching every part of a community.

"(God's laws) are more precious than gold, than much pure gold; they are
sweeter than honey, than honey from the honeycomb. By them your servant is
warned; in keeping them there is great reward (treasure)."
Psalm 19.10-11 NIV

The inner city at times felt like the Wild West, extreme lives living out excessive consequences. We discovered that wounded worshipers in our urban church gravitated toward the Scriptures. Broken lives desired wholeness with boundaries. Over the years I watched with fascination addicts and survivors identifying with the consequences of their actions as reflected in the Scriptures. Honesty and humility happen when an alcoholic hits the bottom. He seeks truth and help. The victim who has lived through pattern trauma becomes ready to heal and grow in God's word when she is "sick and tired of being sick and tired."

Small group Bible studies formed the bedrock of a healing relationship with Christ in our church. The structure of attending the group, loving accountability and support, answered prayer, the transformative presence of the Spirit, the teachings of Christ all contribute to God's system of wholeness. This treasure passage reveals a guide map quality to the Scriptures leading an addict or victim to recovery. The common denominator of the healing work in our church and the successful recovery movements today is Scripture in small groups, God's intimate kingdom community.

But this precious treasure-this light and power that now shine within us-is
held in perishable containers, that is in our weak bodies. So everyone can see
that our glorious power is from God and is not our own. We are pressed on
every side by troubles, but we are not crushed and broken. We are perplexed
but we don't give up and quit. We are hunted down but God never abandons
us. We get knocked down but we get up again and keep going.
2 Corinthians 4:7-9 NLT

When Paul states, *"But this precious treasure . . . . "* he speaks about freedom and transformation of the heart in 2 Corinthians 3.15-4.1. *"Even to this day when Moses is read, a veil covers their hearts. But whenever anyone turns to the Lord, the veil is taken away. Now the Lord is the Spirit, and where the Spirit of the Lord is, there is freedom. And we who with unveiled faces all reflect the Lord's glory, are being transformed into His likeness with an ever increasing glory, which comes from the Lord who is the Spirit. Therefore, since we have this ministry . . . . "* Paul calls this ministry of freedom and transformation "a treasure" in 2 Corinthians 4.7 NIV. This new relationship with God in Christ, the treasure, is experienced in the failure and humanity of the believer. God's power in our frailty proves that the new connection comes from Him and not from man. Paul uses the words "jars of clay" to describe the weak state of the believer. The New Living Translation uses the phrase *"perishable containers, that is in our weak bodies."*

I use the term brokenness in my post modern work. In the weakness of our humanity God demonstrates the power of His grace so much so that *"we are hard pressed on every side, but not crushed; perplexed, but not in despair; persecuted, but not abandoned; struck down, but not destroyed"* 2 Corinthians 4.8-9 NIV. His strength reveals in flawed humanity. I apply this reasoning to the healing of addictions. In brokenness, God's Spirit connects. In the weakness of the addict or victim God brings healing and freedom.

The first step of the twelve in Alcoholics Anonymous admits loss of control, brokenness. At this point of weakness and humility wholeness begins. When addicts and survivors drink in the truth that their limitations and failings actually empower freedom, transformation grips trauma. This treasure passage describes the point of entry for healing addictions and trauma, brokenness. Lives change where His strength and our weakness touch.

Solomon adds a treasure text to our study of brokenness. Literally, the Song of Songs means the greatest or very best of songs. This passage is deep not in what it says, but the results of Solomon's life.

> *How sweet is your love, my treasure, my bride! How much better it is than wine . . . You are like a private garden my treasure, my bride! You are like a spring that no one else can drink from, a fountain of my own.*
> *Song of Solomon 4:10-12 NLT*

Study the Song of Solomon and you will read of passionate love between a man and woman. The inspired words paint a graphic and intimate picture of marital love, definitely for mature audiences only. I never read this book to my kids at bedtime. Breasts, fawns, and sexual passion metaphors feasting on the fruit of pomegranates become a bit too much information for small children. But in these pages you will find the first bloom love of a groom for his bride. Man and woman find belonging and intimacy.

Preceding the Song of Solomon however looms the book of Ecclesiastes like a storm surge with hurricane force winds. In Ecclesiastes Solomon records his life and leadership reflecting hindsight vision on 1000 sexual partners and a life of addictive behavior. He calls his lifestyle "smoke", meaningless, a spitting in the wind. There are two kinds of addictions, substance and process addictions. Both follow the same path with similar results, the death of relationship. Substance addictions are easy to identify; drugs, alcohol, tobacco, food. Process addictions define as sex, unhealthy relationships, rage, control, and countless others. Solomon had a process addiction to sex. 1000 wives and lovers filled his harem. If you do the calculations, the king would need to service about three different women a day every year to keep up with the human inventory. The Scriptures state that Solomon's wives influenced him to worship idols, another process addiction, and turn his back on his faith. The result? Death of relationship with God. I wonder if this passage at the end of a tumultuous life is his best attempt to express sorrow, regret, and apology?

> *Always be clothed in white, and always anoint your head with oil. Enjoy life with your wife whom you love, all the days of this meaningless life that God has given you under the sun. Ecclesiastes 9.8-9.*

The Song of Solomon stands as a sober sentry declaring the danger of addictive relationships. Solomonic metaphors muse lovely and romantic, but underneath lurks a raging rip current of cynicism and remorse. The king could have chosen the treasure of love, but instead carried himself out to sea in a maelstrom of manic sexuality.

Hope surfaces however. You can see a connection to the brokenness passages. Solomon's failure as a husband and leader transform into a rich statement of meaning and purpose for the recovering sex addict. He states at the end of the book in Ecclesiastes 12.13; *Now all has been heard; here is the conclusion of the matter: Fear God and keep His commandments, for this is the whole duty of man.*

After the process addictions of sex, money, and power, Solomon states that meaning emerges as loving God with honor and reverence, keeping between the lines of His conscience and will. Solomon teaches us two things. One, the hard lesson of addictive thinking. Second, the treasure of healing from attachments unearths with honor and love for God.

> *Do not store up for yourselves treasures on earth, where moth and rust destroy, and where thieves break in and steal. But store up for yourselves treasures in heaven, where moth and rust do not destroy, and where thieves do not break in and steal. For where your treasure is, there your heart will be also.*
> *The eye is the lamp of the body. If your eyes are good, your whole body will be full of light. But if your eyes are bad, your whole body will be full of darkness. If then the light within you is darkness, how great is that darkness!*
> *No one can serve two masters. Either he will hate the one and love the other, or he will be devoted to the one and despise the other. You cannot serve both God and Money.*
> *Therefore I tell you, do not worry about your life, what you will eat or drink; or about your body, what you will wear. Is not life more important than food, and the body more important than clothes? Look at the birds of the air; they do not sow or reap or store away in barns, and yet your heavenly Father feeds them. Are you not much more valuable than they? Who of you by worrying can add a single hour to his life?*
>
> *And why do you worry about clothes? See how the lilies of the field grow. They do not labor or spin. Yet I tell you that not even Solomon in all his*

splendor was dressed like one of these. If that is how God clothes the grass of the field, which is here today and tomorrow is thrown into the fire, will he not much more clothe you, O you of little faith? So do not worry, saying, "What shall we eat?" or "What shall we drink?" or "What shall we wear?" For the pagans run after all these things, and your heavenly Father knows that you need them. But seek first His kingdom and His righteousness, and all these things will be given to you as well. Therefore do not worry about tomorrow, for tomorrow will worry about itself. Each day has enough trouble of its own.
Matthew 6:19-25 NIV

This final treasure passage uncovers near the conclusion of Jesus' Sermon on the Mount, Matthew 5-7. He begins the Mount Message with a focus on intimate kingdom community, a treasure theme. He takes His listeners on a journey to discover what it means to live in this relationship. He states that they are blessed, salt and light, and emphasizes loyalty to God as expressed in the Law. This loyalty theme will emerge later. He explores intensely personal matters of anger and reconciliation, the causation of adultery, divorce, oath making, and conflict management. He then addresses the proper motivations for growing deeper.

The treasure passage exposes next. This Scripture preaches like a mini sermon with hook, body and conclusion. The hook is money. The body includes three points on anxiety beginning with, "Don't worry!" He finishes this micro message with a piece on the psychology of projection, a symptom of addictive thinking.

In the hook portion of the treasure micro message, Jesus helps His followers identify the true location of the heart. If Jesus were using contemporary images, He might say that the global position satellite address for the heart would be where resources allocate. The treasure in this passage focuses on surrender to, and concrete connection with Christ. The second piece of the hook again centers on deeper spirituality. If my vision is Christ, then I have the power to see. If the hub of my life blurs, I am spiritually numb. The direct context is money and resource management. Spiritual darkness results from elevating money to the center of attention. The third part of the hook again focuses on resources. If I serve money, then I cannot love God.

The body of this teaching piece aims at the anxieties of the listeners. Jesus spends a considerable amount of discussion on worry over basic life necessities. He does a masterful job of leading the listeners to a point of decision, spot-lighting relationship with God within intimate kingdom community as the solution for worry. The emotional energy behind allegiance to money? Anxiety. Three times Jesus exhorts, "Don't worry!" He closes by exhorting His audience to refocus on seeking " . . . *first His kingdom and His righteousness, and all these things will be given to you as well. Therefore do not worry about tomorrow, for tomorrow will worry about itself. Each day has enough trouble of its own Matthew 6:19-25 NIV.* He wants the hearers to experience that God loves and cares for them. The barrier for this relationship with God is anxiety.

Jesus' message on anxiety comprises a critical piece in my book. One of my sub-theses connects anxiety with addiction. He invites worried listeners to belong to God's kingdom community and relationship with Him as counter-culture to addictive thinking. In this world view God brings peace and freedom making broken people whole. Jesus calls this serenity within an intimate healing community, treasure.

Small Group Bible Study

As you begin your study, make sure you get to know each other. Talk a lot. I enjoy starting with the highlights and lowlights of your week, you know, the good stuff and the meltdowns. Talking about your life is a great privilege. Ask questions, and nurture trust. You will need this as you build your story as a group. Make commitments that your work together will be of the utmost confidentiality. Make a pact to pray for each other daily, call, text, Facebook, or Twitter to connect between gatherings. You are the church, this is the most transformational work you will ever do. Below is a treasure passage you can talk about and then we will start to build your story together.

> *My goal is that they may be encouraged in heart, united in love, so that they have the full riches of complete understanding in order that they may know the mystery of God, namely, Christ in whom are hidden all the treasures of wisdom and knowledge . . . He forgave us all our sins, having cancelled the charge of our legal indebtedness, which stood against us and condemned us; He has taken it away, nailing it to the cross.*
> *Colossians 2.2-3; 13-14 NIV*

There are so many great treasure passages to discuss in your group. This one I think captures the depth of treasure.

1. What is Paul's inspired goal?
2. He sets forth the goal and connects it to a result statement beginning with the words . . . "so that . . . " and a purpose statement beginning with . . . "in order to . . ." What are the result and the purpose?
3. Within this purpose is treasure. Like a diamond treasure has numerous facets. Paul speaks of what two facets?
4. How does Paul end up this treasure passage?

The Good News of Jesus Christ presents to mankind in a story. The Old Testament writers told inspired hi**stories** of God's connection with His people. God's story of touching us possesses power because we connect with the characters and make application with life experiences from our world. We learn lessons through the failures and successes of the good and the bad. Through these inspired accounts the Holy Spirit convicts us of sin, righteousness, and judgment. Paul the Apostle says in 2 Corinthians that the Christians in Corinth are his letter, his story.

> *Your lives are a **letter** written in our hearts; everyone can read it and recognize our good work among you.*
> *2 Corinthians 3.2*

*Clearly, you are a **letter** from Christ showing the result of our ministry among you. This "**letter**" is written not with pen and ink, but with the Spirit of the living God. It is carved not on tablets of stone, but on human hearts.*
2 Corinthians 3.3

So, let's begin to craft your story. Now, to help you start, draw a picture of your family when you were 10 years old. I drew my family sitting at the dinner table. How old were they, what jobs, crises, world politics took place? Share your drawing with your group. Next week we begin the deep work of telling your story. I will also start introducing some friends. They are all truly amazing stories of God's grace. Read their stories and I hope this will help you reflect on your own life. Each week make sure you share your stories with each other after you do your Bible study.

Write Your Story

(Draw your family when you were 10 years old)

SECTION ONE

POST MODERN PAIN

Addictions "R" Us Community Church

I OFTEN THOUGHT we ought to change the name of our inner-city war-zone church plant to Addictions "R" Us Community Church. Here's what I mean. A young cocaine addict met a hooker on Ottawa Street. They had a daughter together. While in rehab, the man broke up with his prostitute girlfriend and fell in love with a woman in his twelve-step program. They came to faith and asked me to marry them. Before the ceremony the bride and groom, wearing matching silk do-rags on their foreheads, informed me that they stationed a guard on the concrete steps in front of the building. The ex-girlfriend, call-girl, vowed to shower the nuptial not with birdseed or bubbles, but bullets. With one eye on my wedding book and another on the glass double doors I led them through their promises. Your preacher faces the doors for a reason . . . to keep lookout for heat–packing prostitutes bent on revenge.

A 70-year-old attendee recovers from crack addiction. He lives in a virtual shack. He sold everything he had to use. Another young crack addict came to faith recently. He sold his wife's golf shoes for a rock . . . seriously? I had lunch with a middle-aged man who desires a deep relationship with God, but does not care for women. He has a history of broken male love relationships. He told me the compulsion for male affection felt like drugs. Although dying a slow death, he wouldn't let go.

An ex-felon, the son of an Australian prostitute, experienced an awesome transformation of life and spirit. His story began when his mother kicked him out of her brothel. The son overheard his mother being hurt in the next room so he attacked her boyfriend. Fact is, the noise did not come from beatings . . . she was working. He landed in America—drugs, gangs, violence. Although now a faithful Christian, he still recovers from a drug deal gone bad. His supplier gave him two choices: "Do you want a beating with a baseball bat or the butt of a gun?" My friend chose the bat.

And the tattoos . . . lots of them. My favorite memory was Walt. Walt rode Harleys. Someone tried to steal his motorcycle so Walt shot the thief and did eight years for second-degree murder. While in prison, his cellmates tattooed most of his body. He literally looked like a convict canvass: spider webs, skulls, and India ink outlines of shapely women. While carved up and colorized behind bars, he also fell in love with Molly, his pen pal. After parole they met in person, began attending our church, and came to faith. While counseling Walt, I asked if I could see his tattoos. Never ask a biker ex-felon to see his tattoos. In one fluid movement Walt stripped off his shirt to expose more ink than I have ever seen on a human being. No one told me in seminary that bikers love to take their clothes off. With the pride of an artist at a New York art show he walked me through his torso-gallery of priceless treasures. On the day of his wedding ceremony I caught Walt smoking in the men's room. Nervous to the bone, he made a great poster child for anxiety. His cigarette didn't upset me because the toxic tobacco exhaust actually made the horrid bathroom smell better. Walt introduced me to his Harley-riding best man, a great guy with a red ponytail down to his hips. He, too, had his shirt off. All across his back and shoulders a huge yellow and red eagle spread its wings. In his nipples dangled earrings, or shall we call them breast rings. He claimed to be a devout Christian. I piously proclaimed relief.

I counseled a young man who had an addiction to women's feet. I still don't get that. He thought a woman's foot more attractive than any other part of her anatomy. Another twenty something could not stay out of adult bookstores. His "chooser" broke, you know, that part of us that makes decisions. He felt compelled to drive into the parking lot. The young man told me that something gripped him, and he found himself stepping through the front doors as though on automatic pilot. One errant board member smoked dope with some of our converts. Groovy church. Find Christ and get loaded.

There were clean addictions, the socially acceptable drugs of choice. These attachments bring adulation, like the millionaire contractor with a broken back who could not stop working. He showed up to work lifting trusses and operating heavy equipment with cracked vertebrae. Other "clean" addictions emerged, like the young wife starving herself to death, or the woman armed with a hatred of men compelled to violent lovers again and again.

In about year three of our ministry, it hit me. Everyone was an addict from board members to visitors! Every counseling appointment I had involved alcohol or other toxic drugs. Every single one. Why in the world would God bring a room full of addicts together? Addicts are rigid, whiny, difficult, self-absorbed. I told myself on numerous occasions that someone made a terrible mistake growing a church this way. You know, violent neighborhood filled with crazy people. Why? The reason is . . . treasure.

You only are a people holy to God, your God; God chose you out of all the
people on Earth as His cherished personal treasure.
Deuteronomy 14.2 MSG

Today God has reaffirmed that you are dearly held treasure just as He
promised a people entrusted with keeping His commandments a people set high
above all other nations that He's made, high in praise, fame, and honor: you're
a people holy to God, your God.
Deuteronomy 26:18 MSG

If you will listen obediently to what I say and keep my covenant, out of all
peoples you'll be my special treasure. The whole Earth is mine to choose from
but you're special; a kingdom of priests, a holy nation.
Exodus 19:5 MSG

The people of Israel were rigid, whiny, difficult, self-absorbed, and . . . the treasure of His Heart. They belonged to God. He loved them. The theme of redemption revolves around God loving us. Look at these words: holy, selected, cherished, personal, dearly held, set high above in praise and honor. We are His treasure. We don't like us. We have criticized, split us, separated us. Though alienated, we belong to God. We discovered this in the inner city. People matter and have supreme value to God. Selected, elected, chosen . . . we are the treasure of His heart.

On a deeper level; God adores addicts. Our attachments have the potential to make us real and honest, loving God deeply. Hang out with a room full of recovering alcoholics. They are the most honest bunch you will ever meet. The pursuit of our drug of choice tracks the search for intimacy with God. Not far from your home a bar boldly advertises "spirits". In neon letters, for the world to see, the tavern owner declares every drink opens the door for a spiritual journey. The quest for alcohol, drugs, sex, thinness, affirmation, or work underscores the search for Jesus Christ. Addiction seeks treasure; the deeper, the richer, that which you wrap your arms around when hope dissolves into despair. Jesus Christ in an intimate healing community of people touches and heals the most profound pain of the human heart.

What launches addictive behavior and how is it possible that God brought wholeness to post modern people in the 'hood? Let's go to the beginning. Genesis 1-3. The Bible shows this beautiful balance of man, woman, and the Creator. God also gives boundaries in this perfect panorama. Look at this passage of Scripture. God said, *"You can eat from any tree in the Garden, except from the Tree of Knowledge of Good and Evil – do not eat from it, the moment that you eat from that tree – you're dead"* Genesis 2:16-17 MSG.

Every good parent gives loving limits to their children. God created boundaries with balanced relationship to enjoy intimate community. The tempter approached Eve and said, "Are you sure – did God really say that you would die if you ate the fruit of that tree? Is it really true?" Normally we interpret the "sin" in this foundational story as pride. Adam and Eve desire to be like God, and the tempter plays upon that pride. But something else gripped them before hubris hammered the first family. The tempter drives a wedge between Eve and her God. Can she trust Him? Does the Creator really have her best interests at heart? The intimate connection now reels on its heels out of balance. The word group for temptation and trial means distress, worry, anxiety. Take your right index finger and place it on the top of your left hand. Push down lightly. That pressure you feel now impacts the nerves in the hand communicating to the brain that imbalance entered. Your left hand responds by pushing back trying to maintain its position. The strain you feel in your hand and the communication in the brain we call imbalance or anxiety. Simple. The enemy pressures Eve. He coerces, imbalance grips her. Responding without faith and reason she pressures her husband. Soon their choices spread beyond them and addictive, destructive behaviors follow. In the opening nine chapters of the book of Genesis, we read of broken and blended families, alcoholism, and the first victim of sexual assault. Adam and Eve's imbalance creates a domino effect. Addiction follows anxiety. This is called anxiety reaction (Steinke). The beginning of hurt in your life starts with pressure and its result, anxiety.

Anxiety reaction operates like this. Three centers in the brain form distinct responses to stimuli – the first is the fight and flight center. You find this at the base of the brain comprising the cerebellum and the top of the spinal cord. Have you ever been startled? A state trooper swoops behind your errant vehicle, red and blue lights pulsate instant panic, blood pressure spikes, sweat seeps, and you frantically seek registration and insurance proof. That's the fight and flight response of anxiety. The second axis forms the feelings center. This area locates in the mid section of the brain and composes the hypothalamus, pituitary, amygdala, and hippocampus. The hypothalamus is one of the busiest parts of the brain. It contains the primary center for emotions and drives such as sex, anger, body temperature, hormones, sleeping, eating, drinking, pain and pleasure. When you say hypothalamus, think thermostat. Its primary role creates balance. Do you feel hot? The hypothalamus cools you down regulating blood pressure, perspiration, and breathing. The hypothalamus receives numerous nerve inputs telling your brain when you have had too much to eat, light and dark information, and can even register toxins in the spinal fluid triggering a vomit response.

The pituitary secretes growth hormone and directs glands like the thyroid, adrenal, ovaries and testes. The amygdala look like two almonds at the lower end of the hippocampus regulating feelings of aggression and sex. When this area of the brain suffers damage, patients can become lethargic and dispassionate. The hippocampus looks like two horns curving back from the amygdala. The hippocampus controls pleasure and aversion stimuli and some long term memory. For example, it converts short term memory into long term memory. If this area is damaged, the victim cannot form new memories. He lives in a bizarre world where new experiences fade away though old memories endure. When anxiety reacts in the feeling center, intense emotions result like sex, pleasure, anger, and rage.

Look at Eve's reply to the pressure of the tempter in Genesis 3. She reacts not from faith and reason, but from emotions connecting to "beauty and appetite," originating from the feeling center.

> *The woman was convinced. She saw that the tree was beautiful and its fruit looked delicious, and she wanted the wisdom it would give her. So she took some of the fruit and ate it. Then she gave some to her husband, who was with her, and he ate it, too. At that moment their eyes were opened, and they suddenly felt shame at their nakedness. So they sewed fig leaves together to cover themselves.*
> *Genesis 3.6 NLT*

The third center of response is the cerebral cortex where faith and reason take shape. The faith center comprises three fourths of the brain's mass. Kind of gives you an idea where God loves to operate in our lives. When anxiety enters, it reacts with the fight, flight and feeling areas of the brain, and does not engage the center for faith and reason in the cerebral cortex (Steinke). Faith and relationship with God must be chosen in the imbalance of temptation and trial. This explains why alcohol and drug abuse weaken relationship with God. These chemicals anesthetize the cerebral cortex undermining faith, reasoning, and listening to God. This clarifies the behavior of good people when under stress they can respond with anger, fear, and intense emotion rather than faith and reason. This explains why at times I run, fight, and focus on what I feel rather than on the goodness of God.

All react to anxiety. We have a dog family. Lori and I love dogs and have had dogs ever since our honeymoon. Dogs are not animals to us. They are our people . . . children really. Our pooch possesses a people name. He sleeps with us, eats with us—he is our son. My wife's mother, Loretta, brought her Yorkshire terrier, Shandy, to visit. My dog–loving family sits sipping coffee in the kitchen. I approach Shandy, who lounges on my wife's lap. I bend down and talk that cute baby dialect you speak with infants. Shandy and I begin kissing. She licks my beard and laps my lips—the cutest thing. We kiss and I converse with her in baby phonics while smiling Lori tenderly holds the dog. We look like a Thomas Kincaid painting. Then Lori speaks, "You might not want to kiss her, darling . . . Shandy was juuuust eating dog poop a few minutes ago!" Anxiety. My hypothalamus kicks in and I bend over to lose my lunch with a vomit response. Then, I spend the next few minutes chasing my wife through the kitchen, trying to kiss her in return. My anxious illogic, "If I die from e-coli, she goes too!"

In the Sermon on the Mount Jesus calls His followers to choose an unanxious life. He states that your Heavenly Father knows your needs and will give you what you require day to day if you choose faith in Him and belong to His healing kingdom community.

Jesus understands the power of anxiety and its thorough treatment in the Scriptures. If you have ever contemplated the impact of worry in the Bible simply look at the references to "fear". Over 500 times in the Bible the words fear and afraid appear. On the one hand fear connects to reverence, on the other fear reflects the process of anxiety reaction and worry. Trace temptation and trial throughout Scripture from the Garden and patriarchs in Genesis, the trials of the kings and people of Israel, the temptation of Christ in the wilderness, and the persecution of the early church and you have one of the most comprehensive themes in the Bible. What Christ does to redeem mankind in the midst of temptation, anxiety, imbalance, and fear forms a major mega-theme in God's word.

Some translations use the word worry in Jesus' sermon, which derives from the German word, *wergan,* meaning "to strangle." In the Greek language, the word worry is more dynamic. It means to "split the mind". When anxiety grips us, it splits the mind from faith and reason and operates in the regions of fight, flight, and feelings. Jesus understood this thousands of years ago when He said to unearth the treasure of loving God with faith and reason, not anger, fear, and emotion.

When Jesus used the term "split the mind", He spoke accurately about the effect of anxiety at the cellular level. Each neuron in our brain exists as a living entity. It is born, reproduces, takes in nourishment, expels waste, has purpose, takes initiative, communicates with other neurons, then dies. Communities of neurons organize the brain. How these groups of neurons respond to each other explains brain activity.

Because God hard wired our brains for balance, neurons exchange chemical information through neurotransmitters and neuroreceptors to maintain homeostasis. The connection points for this information at any neuron range from 20,000 to 200,000. Alcohol, drugs, caffeine and nicotine powerfully affect this interaction. If the average neuron has 20,000 connections to 10 billion to 1 trillion neurons, this means that the brain connects at 500 trillion points. A supercomputer counting 100 connections a second would require 10-15 thousand years to add up the total neurological contacts for one brain. Every communication of thought, feeling, and behavior creates a supremely complex process (May, p. 70).

Enter the pressure of trials. God designed our system for stability. Imbalance causes delicate cellular shifts to take place. Three neurological responses restore balance in the brain. The first cellular response is called feedback. You have a conversation with a friend; it's interesting and you lean forward, "tell me more."

The talker converses too loud and you ask, "Calm down!" The conversation deteriorates to a whisper and you respond, "Speak up." Feedback between neurons creates balance by adjusting the levels of chemical transmission between neurons. Stability results.

If imbalance from anxiety continues, neurons habituate. Brain chemicals forcefully stop messages between cells. Ladies, have you ever noticed that after talking to your husband for 15 minutes, you ask him what he thinks about your feelings and he turns to you and says, "What feelings?" Because anxiety reacts, neuro-chemicals release to block your conversation from processing in the brain. The forceful cancellation of messages between neurons is called habituation. Neurons adjust to the new level of anxiety to create balance. This is the same thing that happens when you press your index finger onto the top of your hand, after awhile you don't feel the pressure because cells have habituated. Or, when walking on the beach, you notice after awhile that you "tuned out" the sound of the waves. This too is habituation and it happens all the time without our knowledge. In terms of recovery from addiction brain cells become tolerant. As a result, our unstable system demands more alcohol, unhealthy relationships, drugs, nicotine or caffeine to create the same soothing effect.

The human brain cannot habituate forever. If pressure and imbalance continue, a new stability must be created. This is called attachment, or addiction. Anxiety increases and reacts. Brain cells adapt their makeup; neurotransmitters and receptors chemically transform to create a new balance. Chemical composition of cells changes, and anxiety diminishes. We literally become different people. We look the same, but our neurological make up morphs. Personality changes permanently. Stress the system and withdrawal, irritability, moodiness, worry result. We become rigid, whiny, difficult, and self absorbed. Multiple systems of neurons within the brain engage impacting each other. Jesus said it, the mind splits. Attachments and addictions rule our lives. The garden repeats: imbalance, worry, anxiety reaction, inappropriate control, and death of relationships (May, pp. 64-90).

Let's go deeper into the anatomy of anxiety leading to addiction. There are four types of anxiety: neurotic, historical, existential, and father hunger. These anxieties find commonality with all humans.

Neurotic anxiety results from inner contradictions, painful memories, and impulsive desires. In families where emotions are forbidden children may stuff their anger or sexual feelings for the sake of belonging. When anger or sex emerge later in life, anxiety escalates. This anxiety acts as a defensive response to keep these banned emotions from the conscious mind. Alcohol and other consciousness altering drugs numb neurotic anxiety.

Historical anxiety surfaces from crises of culture. Post moderns feel this profoundly. Two jet planes impale themselves into the World Trade Center's twin towers. The enormity of murder suicide in grandiose proportion on American soil rocks the security of everyone who watched the disaster. One out of every ten Americans is killed in utero. Video game junkies in trench coats commit cold blooded murder in a Colorado school. Not far away the leader of one of the largest mega churches in America quits after confessions of sexual indiscretion and illegal drug infatuation. A few weeks after the pastoral resignation, a gunman opens fire on the same church campus. Where do we find safety? If the unborn find no haven, and danger lurks within the local expression of the church, where does hope find us? Historical anxiety starts in the harsh truth of current events.

You wonder what your purpose in life is. On your 48th birthday you do the math and realize that in another half century you are dead. You catch a cold, your cousin contracts cancer, a younger friend dies of a heart attack. Yet at the same time you sense a hunger to live above sickness and death. Immortality and life everlasting are a good deal. Last week I visited a friend in the hospital. He had just died from terminal lung cancer. An hour later I met with a young couple for their wedding rehearsal. Tears, joy, pain, hope within the scope of one hour. Inside you feel a moral oughtness. You know the difference between right and wrong. Yet, choices are made to deceive, and hurt the closest relationships. Existential anxiety ranges from the math of mortality, the tears of joy and despair, to the tension of conscience.

Finally, father hunger is the innate need to connect with God (Maine, p. xvi). Cemented within all humanity pulses a passion to connect with the fatherhood of God. When the connection is clear, we find balance and strength in life. If relationship with God suffers, a devastating war of worry wages. When disconnected, relational dread gnaws through His fatherhood and trauma bites deeper.

Neurotic, historical, existential, and father hunger anxieties connect to our addictions. Trace the drugs and broken relationships back far enough and you will find anxiety and worry as the catalyst (Clinebell, pp. 264-267).

What happened in the 'hood? Why did post moderns find help and healing? Let's look at the first family in Genesis and examine the points of entry for wholeness.

Adam and Eve give in to the pressure of temptation, imbalance disrupts, and they respond without faith and reason. Intimate community disintegrates. Shame enters and they hide.

Toward evening, they heard the Lord God walking about in the garden, so they hid themselves among the trees. And the Lord God called to Adam –
"Where are you?"
Genesis 3:8-9 NIV

Anxiety leads to a reaction of fight or flight. All of this together is felt as shame. Having neither IQ nor rationale shame holds love back, secretes itself from the wonder of grace and presence of God. Shame results as the emotional aftermath when anxiety reacts to threatened relational ties (Middleton-Moz, p. 15). The

Scriptures state that they covered their disgrace and hid. God pursues man and woman in their shame. After teaching this passage one Sunday, a teenager handed me a cartoon she drew of Adam and Eve in the garden. Adam sported a fig leaf Speedo and Eve wore a one-piece leaf outfit. Above Eve's head was a cartoon balloon. Eve implores her husband saying, "Adam, do these leaves make me look fat?" When we feel anxiety and respond out of fight and flight and not faith, debilitating shame follows and we disappear relationally. Shame takes cover and conceals. Addicts numb this pain with chemicals or other non-substance attachments.

The Lord God made garments of skin for Adam and his wife and clothed them.
Genesis 3.21 NIV

Perhaps the most beautiful words in Scripture; God engages and then covers their disgrace. He cares for them. He does what they cannot do themselves. This act of grace casts a vision for the tenderness of Jesus Christ on the cross. He seeks us in our shame and takes the rap for our sin and attachments with the shedding of His blood. Christ does for us what we cannot begin to imagine . . . he covers our disgrace with grace. The New Testament adorns clothing terminology as well.

Since God chose you to be the Holy people whom He loves, you must clothe
yourselves with tenderhearted mercy, kindness, humility, gentleness, and
patience. You must make allowance for each other's faults and forgive the
person who offends you. Remember, the Lord forgave you, so you must forgive
others. And the most important piece of clothing you must wear is love. Love is
what binds us all together in perfect harmony.
Colossians 3:12-14 NLT

Jesus Christ is our treasure. He pursues hurt sin-filled people covering shame with tenderness, kindness, and gentleness. He forgives. Anxiety absconds. His love reverses relational disappearance and emotional sabotage. Balance emerges. The healing of trauma begins. We are His treasure and we belong.

By the way, Biker Walt and tattoos look great. He lives in Chicago with his beautiful mail bride Molly. They visited not long ago, to introduce me to their non-tattooed son, Walt Jr., with a shoulder-length blonde ponytail. They also wanted to report how they are . . . how good God is.

Small Group Bible Study

Reconnect by talking over your highlights and lowlights. Did you call each other this week? Did you pray daily? If not, recommit yourselves and go for it this week ok? Share your family picture of when you were 10 years old. Now, let's examine a passage from the chapter this week.

If you will listen obediently to what I say and keep my covenant, out of all peoples you'll be my special treasure. The whole Earth is mine to choose from but you're special; a kingdom of priests, a holy nation.
Exodus 19:5 MSG

1. Your story builds around the attitude God has of you. You are His treasure among all the people on the planet. What does that mean to you?

2. Because you belong to Him, God challenges you to live a certain way. Discuss this passage and what does it mean to you and your community?

Since God chose you to be the Holy people whom He loves, you must clothe yourselves with tenderhearted mercy, kindness, humility, gentleness, and patience. You must make allowance for each other's faults and forgive the person who offends you. Remember, the Lord forgave you, so you must forgive others. And the most important piece of clothing you must wear is love. Love is what binds us all together in perfect harmony.
Colossians 3:12-14 NLT

Writing Your Story, Healing Your Heart

The anxieties of your life connect to your family story. I will cite Keith to help you get started. After you read about his life, write out the story of your parents. Try to connect to their anxieties.

Keith's Story

My name is Keith. Many of my friends can say their father was a great athlete, a mentor in hunting, fishing, or maybe a community leader. My father was a sexual predator. The story gets worse. He was also an ordained professional minister in a mainline denomination. I grew up in liturgical church services watching him preach in clerical garb on Sundays and raging on Mondays. Although the full revelation of his serial sexuality did not emerge until recently, as a child I noticed he seemed to do the math on connecting with women constantly. I recall the pornography he read, the inappropriate remarks about sex at the dinner table, and the lack of prayer and Scripture in a pastor's home. He told me once that sex with someone you are not married to is legitimate as long as you love them. In hindsight he reflected on his own indiscretions. I did not fully comprehend it, but I intuited something was wrong.

My single grandmother gave birth to my father on a mid western farm. Illegitimate sons embarrassed small depression era communities. I recall once he sat our family down and lamented that he was a "bastard" son. I did not understand that. He grew up with a deep sense of shame for a story he could not control. His emotionally detached mother married a violent abusive husband. When my father turned 14 years old, his mother warned him to leave home because she felt certain the step father would murder my dad. He joined the Navy at the end of World War 2 finding himself a willing participant in the Asian sex trade. While on ship at Christmas time, he watched a movie with Jimmy Stewart whose character lost his family and fatherhood. In his despair the character turned to God. My father claims a spiritual conversion.

Upon his return to the United States he enrolled in a deeply conservative Bible college to study for the ministry in a fundamentalist church. He met my mother and they married. One of my mother's first recollections of his sexual obsession came when he refused to come to the hospital when she gave birth to me. She saw him working illicit angles with the baby sitter. Becoming disillusioned with the rigidity of this fundamentalist denomination, he quit and allied himself with a more progressive movement. He enrolled in a seminary where they taught him the relativity of truth, the errancy of Scripture, and situational ethics. I recall one of his favorite statements, "If it feels good, do it. If you can't be with the one you love . . . love the one you are with." He once tried to negotiate with my mother to have an open marriage, this means sexual relations with whomever he wished . . . with her consent. She refused . . . he continued the predation. He took his addiction seriously. We don't know exactly how many women in the ministry he had affairs with, but we can confirm the young widow he counseled in the aftermath of her husband's death, the organist, the music pastor's wife, and numerous women he counseled. His position of power put him within striking distance of vulnerable women who looked to him for guidance. His last affair was not his final transgression. A young woman in another church in a different city succumbed to his addiction. They had an affair, he divorced my mother, married the most recent victim and then moved onto another church. But the trauma did not stop there. The new wife had a daughter from her former marriage. The serial sexuality continued to abuse his stepdaughter. I have been told by a counselor of abuse survivors that sexual predators have over 100 victims in their lifetime. I fear to do this math for my father.

Write Out Your Parent's Story

Healing Survivors of Trauma

(Rated R)

IN THE INNER city we didn't set record attendance figures and budget numbers. We experienced good music and people complimented the preaching, but the deeper-richer facet of life in the 'hood was wholeness for the human heart. Shame-filled addicted lives found help and healing. There were more; survivors of every kind of trauma imaginable.

A twisted father serially raped his three daughters. A woman, surrounded by people she trusted, was violated by a dog. A man addicted to cocaine beat his wife and did time in the Jackson penitentiary. As I counseled him, we discovered that his shame originated from boyhood when an uncle raped him. A sick father sexually abused his daughter through childhood. On the eve of her wedding a brother had his way with her. A woman came from a deeply fundamentalist family. Her father held a church office on a deacon board. He served as a double agent ritually assaulting his daughter sexually. A woman was raped by her father and a minister; her mother . . . a lesbian. She approached me one Sunday after service and said, "Glen, I think I had an affair." She found semen and could not recall the donor. She often found herself in remote locations with no memory. This is typical for dissociative identity disorder (formerly known as multiple personality disorder) caused by sexual assault. I counseled survivors whose voices differed from one conversation to another. I keep a "thank you" greeting card in my file from a little girl. The handwriting is messy and simple. The author of that card was over 30 when she wrote.

One Sunday morning after service a woman proclaimed, "Pastor Glen, I have a colostomy bag because of the rough sex I had with my boyfriend." They don't teach you this in seminary. Where do you find words of comfort in a prayer manual for S and M? One day I had three counseling appointments. First, a victim of serial rape who abused her children. The next was a woman ambushed outside her home by a jealous lover. Third, a man who beat his head with his hands. I restrained him so that he would not injure himself. He could not recover from his father committing shotgun suicide.

During the twelve years of serving in the 'hood every woman I counseled told a story of trauma. I tell other pastors about our church in the inner city and they look at me like deer in headlights. Massive addiction and trauma. But the church grew in a cruel neighborhood full of traumatized people. Addicts did not find recovery because of our beautiful building. It was a dump. Survivors didn't experience belonging and grace because of purpose statements, and mega church strategies. Wholeness happened because of the deeper, the richer . . . treasure.

> *Today God has reaffirmed that you are dearly held treasure just as He*
> *promised a people entrusted with keeping His commandments a people set high*
> *above all other nations that He's made, high in praise, fame, and honor: you're*
> *a people holy to God, your God.*
> *Deuteronomy 26:18 MSG*

Our ragtag group of religious refugees in the 'hood is the treasure of God's heart. He loves addicts and survivors. The crowd that followed Christ? Drunks, extortionists, and call girls. The followers who broke chains, streaked cemeteries, the multiple personalities . . . His treasure. God does not cause our pain, and neither will He waste it. God loves those whom He has chosen to call His own.

In order to heal victimization in the post modern era we must first understand it. Let's examine the nature of trauma. The first kind of trauma harms because of the absence of good things. In the brain, neurons most affected by these kinds of wounds are found in the feeling center. We hurt when reminded of good things we did not receive. For example, someone who fell short of parent expectations might find himself driven to perfectionism, obsessed with achieving success to the point that he may sabotage his own spouse or children. Another might find himself unable to be alone, bouncing from one relationship to the next in search of someone who will make him feel accepted.

In order to understand the pervasive nature of trauma I will list numerous symptoms of victimization. The range of definition impacts. Wounds which damage because of the things withheld include:

> Parents who don't cherish, celebrate, or encourage a child to share his thoughts and feelings. This list also includes: absence of non-sexual physical nurturing, arms to embrace, and a willingness to let go, respect for boundaries, not receiving age appropriate limits and having those

limits enforced in ways that do not call value into question, not being given adequate food, clothing, shelter, medical and dental care, not being taught how to do hard things, how to solve problems, develop persistence, and to finish projects, not given opportunities to develop personal resources and talents. In other words, a child is not allowed to be (Friesen, p. 44).

These traumas form the root of imbalance, anxiety, and addiction. They drive the struggle we have experiencing belonging with God and family.

The second area of woundedness affects memory. They cause pain not because of their absence, but their presence. These traumas occur on a continuum of severity, but there is no abuse lesser or greater than any other. A mugging victim or person repeatedly put down by a parent suffers trauma. Each experiences desecration, exposure and powerlessness in both situations. The intensity of the emotions differs, but both people feel shaken and distraught. These kinds of traumas can be physical or sexual. Physical abuse includes: slapping, pulling hair, shaking, hitting, kicking, hysteria producing tickling, spitting, and discipline resulting in marks or bruises. Sexual abuse includes two types, verbal and physical. Verbal abuse includes threats, comments on a person's shape, and sharing sexual experiences with children. Physical sexual abuse involves more than intercourse or rape. It includes exposure to porn and sexually provocative images. Physical abuse can also comprise touching to arouse the abuser, exposure, and being photographed. There are estimates that by age eighteen, one in four woman and one in six men will have experienced some form of sexual trauma (Friesen, pp. 44-47). Nearly thirty-one percent of all women have reported physical and or sexual abuse by their husbands or boyfriends at some point in their lives. One third of churchgoers and folks at the local pub have been abused (Office of Women's Health, 2000). This is profound. The men and women in your local church have experienced trauma at the same rate as non-church going victims.

Other traumas which harm us because of their presence in our lives include parental abandonment including death. Unresolved family conflicts, torture, serial trauma, and witnessing abuse also cause trauma. Each of these wounds damages, contributing to the process of anxiety reaction and addiction (Bolthouse).

One phenomenon we witnessed in the inner city is the tendency for victims to repeat patterns of abuse. Dr. Basal Vander Kolk, a psychiatrist and expert in the field of trauma and recovery, discovered that people who have been through ongoing suffering, like war veterans, often become mercenaries and re-traumatize themselves. They survive the horror of war and yet return to it. His research also found that survivors of trauma often become prostitutes and re-victimize themselves. The child who grows up in an abusive home filled with yelling and screaming then marries the same kind of person.

In his research, Vander Kolk found that neurons, during periods of anxiety and imbalance, release endogenous opiods, the brain's equivalent to morphine. These chemicals, under tremendous stress, act as an anesthesia until the crisis ceases. In time neurons adapt and the victim becomes addicted to the anesthetic feelings in the crisis. Vander Kolk discovered, after viewing a 15-minute violent movie, up to 8 milligrams of the morphine equivalent release into the brain. Every 15-minute interval in which crisis engages, the brain releases morphine-type chemicals. The result? it's not that we want crisis in our life . . . we crave it (Clinton, p. 111).

Let's look at what happens when we face trauma. The first is this: An erosion of personality, the loss of personhood. When we hurt deeply, we begin to identify that the trauma is us and we lose our identity. Survivors who have gone through profound grief experience this. Depression intensifies, grief deepens and personal uniqueness disappears. They feel as though they *are* the trauma. A friend of mine spoke with me about a messy divorce. He said that things were improving in his life, but his friends ask him, "When do we get our old friend back?" Trauma erodes identity when we go through successive events of suffering (Herman, p. 86).

Then, the Rambo syndrome. Sylvester Stallone portrayed a Vietnam vet who returns to civilian life. Rambo's own countrymen betray him, attempt to kill him, and he strikes back. Seen pictures of Rambo? The bloody headband, the sleeveless shirt, the M-16, and the belt of bullets across his chest. He looks like a twentieth-century gladiator. This is the image of what happens when trauma changes us. We dig in, fight back, and we do life alone (Herman, p. 59).

The third aspect of trauma is called psychic numbing. It presents as an altered state of consciousness; i.e. the loss of moral compass, integrity meltdown, a paralysis of purity. Not only can it happen to individuals, it can happen to whole communities of people.

In the Mi Lai Massacre a handful of American soldiers murdered hundreds of innocent Vietnamese. An entire year elapsed before a witness came forward to report the atrocity. This is psychic numbing, the loss of conscience. It can happen to a country. Take the 60's; the death of John F. Kennedy, Cold War anxiety, the sexual revolution. Then war. Body counts on TV, demonstrations, Kent State, Martin Luther King, Bobby Kennedy, Watergate. After all this Roe vs. Wade (Herman, p. 45). Every two weeks more children in America are aborted than the entire casualty list of the Vietnam War (Guttmacher, 2001). Moral compass disappears.

Finally, abandonment from God. Survivors perceive that God caused the pain and if He authentically cared He would help them avoid the emotional aftermath. Ever feel abandoned by God? You've gone through a series of events in your life and it feels as though God's absent, and if He were present, He doesn't care. These characteristics profile what happens when trauma wounds (Herman, pp. 52-56).

The transformation of addicts and survivors in the inner city happened in small group Bible studies of healing people. One of the core values of our ministry, therapists call it the talking cure (Herman, p. 12). Church can't be about attending an hour-long service on a Sunday morning, residing in a luxury chair and enjoying musical programming. Deeper spirituality heals the heart. God tenderly touches the trauma of life in small groups of healing Christians.

Look at this passage from Acts. This Scripture gives a blueprint of early church life:

> *They were strong about the teaching of the apostles, and koinonia, the breaking*
> *of bread, and prayers . . . . They followed a daily discipline of worship*
> *followed by meals at home. Every meal a celebration,*
> *exuberant and joyful as they praised God.*
> *Acts 2:42 Greek New Testament and the NIV*

A powerful word unearths in this text – koinonia–meaning intimate, caring community. Luke borrowed this vocabulary from Plato. Koinonia to Plato formed the basis of salvation for the entire universe. This holds the cosmos together . . . what brings wholeness . . . a gracious God in real community (Kittel Vol. IX, p. 799). Here God listens, His Spirit works to help and heal. First century Christianity composed a larger community made up of small groups in house churches. They loved corporate worship but always near in curative intimate relationships. Here Christians found wholeness in relationship to God and each other. The core of trauma removes power and disconnects the victim from God and others. Intimate biblical community restores what addiction and trauma remove; empowerment through His presence, connection with His spirit in community.

Over the years I watched survivors of the most horrible trauma imaginable. Those that heal and grow choose nearness in small groups. Those that continue the addiction and trauma isolate and detach. This is the deeper, the richer, that which you wrap your arms around when hope dissolves into despair . . . an intimate healing Christian community whose treasure is Christ.

Small Group Bible Study

Reconnect as a group. Start with prayer. Hold hands. This is a treasure. Look at this passage of Scripture together as a group. Can you read it from several different translations? Discuss what the early church was like.

> *They were strong about the teaching of the apostles, and koinonia, the breaking*
> *of bread, and prayers. . . . They followed a daily discipline of worship*
> *followed by meals at home. Every meal a celebration, exuberant and joyful as*
> *they praised God.*
> *Acts 2:42 Greek New Testament and the NIV*

1. Discuss what the early church was strong about.

2. Is your faith community strong or weak in what areas? How can we grow deeper to become the church?

3. What were the early disciplines of the church? Again, in what areas does your faith community show strength and weakness? How do we grow forward?

4. What did Plato have to say about koinonia? What is it?

5. In this passage describe what treasure is to God. I count 7 descriptors of treasure. What does this mean for your faith community? What does this mean as you reach your community of family and friends for Christ?

> *Today God has reaffirmed that you are dearly held treasure just as He*
> *promised a people entrusted with keeping His commandments a people set high*
> *above all other nations that He's made, high in praise, fame, and honor:*
> *you're a people holy to God, your God.*
> *Deuteronomy 26:18 MSG*

Writing Your Story, Healing Your Heart

This week write your story of hurt, betrayal and pain. Go slow. This will require a great deal of confidentiality. You may pass and not share your story if you do not feel safe. Read about Marta . . . perhaps this will help. One more piece to add to your group life. There are three kinds of truthful answers to give or write about. There are truthful answers, more truthful answers, and brutally true answers. A truthful answer is like, "Yes I have a story of hurt and pain." A more truthful answer could be, "My story of hurt and pain involves my dad and his affairs." A brutally true answer is, "My father assaulted me growing up with rage and violent behavior. His addictions inspired a life of medicating pain and denial which impact me to this day." Does all that make sense? When you give an answer, share the brutally true answer or wait until you can. Hold each other accountable to be brutally truthful ok? Write your story below. Be brutally honest.

Marta's Story

The sexual abuse in my life started from the time of my first memories which was about four or five. The trauma happened by our family friend's older boys. It only continued for a couple years before my family moved. At the time, I did not have the sense of what was happening nor did I have any idea that my sexuality had been opened up at a really young age.

When my family moved to a different city I must have carried a tattoo on my forehead marked "victim," because before I was ten I began being sexually abused by a thirty-three year old man. I had a better idea of right and wrong so when this trauma began I felt a lot of guilt and shame. It seemed like it was my fault that the sexual abuse was happening. I kept the secret to myself; I didn't want to tell any of my friends and especially my parents. The trauma happened periodically for about two years.

In a spurt where the abuser was not around, one of my neighbors took me to a Vacation Bible School where I heard about Jesus for the first time in my life and I accepted Him into my heart. When the abuser reappeared in my life, I knew I was a Christian and that I couldn't do those things which he had made me do. It was only after I saw him a couple times that the trauma started again. This time the sexual abuse was more aggressive and scary. I knew I had to tell my friends. I told a couple of friends and they encouraged me to tell my parents. I told my mom and we ended up filing charges against the abuser and he was convicted and sent to prison.

This marked the end of trauma but the beginning of the evaluation to the damage of my heart. I was twelve and just entering into adolescence, this was a confusing and tough stage of life. I went to counseling and it didn't seem to help at all. My outlet at the time was sports, I was really good at them and it gave me a way to escape my heart. Somewhere in this time of raging adolescent hormones is when I started to notice an innocent attraction to the same sex.

Once I reached high school the confusion about my sexuality only escalated and by the end of my freshman year of high school I had my first sexual encounter with a girl. I continued to date guys and be with girls. I was completely living a double life.

During my first same sex encounter the moment she crossed the line with me I felt a rush that I had never felt before. I very quickly became addicted to that same rush and intense high. I suppose the rush was brought on by knowing what I was doing was wrong and at any moment could be caught. As time went on the intense highs were met with ultimate lows. The times of ultimate lows were the scariest and loneliest times in my life, almost unbearable. Even though I have never tried any drugs, living this lifestyle was a type of drug. I would go from girl to girl looking for the selfish highs, trying to ignore the miserable lows of guilt and shame of knowing it was wrong and God did not approve of my actions.

As a sophomore I made my best attempt to stop my homosexual tendencies. I would go to my non-denominational church and pray for God to take away my desires, but by Monday I was back to doing what I always did. My only glimmer of hope was when I went on a mission's trip and the Holy Spirit touched me. I stayed cleaned from same sex relationships for a period of time, but my desires and unhealed brokenness always got the better of me and I went back to same sex relationships. This struggle continued through high school and into college. I felt as though I could never change and this is when I really started to believe in the possibility that I was born gay.

In college I played basketball and toward the end of my freshman year I hit the lowest point of my life. I was in a secret relationship with a girl on my team and my coach found out. My coach pulled me into his office and told me to just come out of the closet and be gay. He knew I was a Christian and told me I could be gay and be a Christian. I told him that I knew in my heart I couldn't do that and from that point on I knew I had to make the choice to be gay or not.

Over the next month my life began to fall apart at the seams. I didn't even know who I was anymore. I wasn't the person everyone loved and wanted to be around. I had become crazy with my emotional highs and lows that I didn't even like being around me. I was a mess. When I looked in the mirror I couldn't believe this is who I had become. I thought to myself this couldn't be the true me. I knew my only hope of change would be to turn to God. There had to be someway He could change me.

One of my teammates had been going to a church and raved about the people she had met and relationships she had built. So I asked my teammate to set up a meeting with a lady she had become close with. I told her about my same sex relationships and how I wanted out. She hooked me up with a Pastor's wife that had gone through same sex relationships. The Pastor's wife spoke the cold hard truth of my situation and I walked away from that meeting sad and unable to detach from my current relationship. But her words haunted me and by the end of the summer I had ended my relationship. Entering my sophomore year of college, I went to church regularly and stayed clear of any sexual relationships. I still had the desire for girls but I just didn't act on it. I prayed earnestly for God to take my desires away, but what I didn't know was there was brokenness inside me eating at my core that needed to be healed.

All my best efforts and understanding were as if I had been putting a band aid on a festering wound. The trauma scabbed over for a brief amount of time but it always to find a way to tear open and bleed again. I would be back to acting on my same sex desires and feeling hopeless with endless amounts of guilt and shame. I needed an encounter from God in an intimate and real way.

I wish I could say that my process was overnight, but it wasn't, it was long and painful but worth every moment. To start my journey of change, one of the pastors on staff began counseling with me. With the help of Jesus through the Holy Spirit, I was able to dive into places of my heart I had never been before. It was scary to go there, but Jesus always met me there and healed everything I offered to Him. Counseling helped me to identify thought patterns that led me to same sex conclusions. Many times I felt vulnerable and raw, but I never felt abandoned. I was renewing my mind to God's thoughts and replacing old thoughts with new ones. Jesus' love covered me in a way that words cannot describe.

In the first few weeks of starting counseling I believed that I would learn to suppress and deal with the homosexual desires but I wouldn't ever be completely rid of them. I am so relieved to say that statement was a wrong belief. Though my process was long, it was through God's Word, counseling, and healthy same sex friendships I was able to overcome and defeat the desire for a sexual same sex relationship. I no longer struggled with thoughts or desires of a homosexual lifestyle. God's love had prevailed and He had healed my deep wounds, the scars of memories were all that remained.

After the initial excitement of overcoming homosexuality, I continually experienced God's faithfulness and grace in different ways. The biggest experience happened after three and a half years of being clean and working my process. My friend Dan and I had been friends for three years and he knew all about me. God opened our eyes and hearts to each other and we started dating. After nine short months of dating we were married. During our engagement we talked a lot about my past issues and I expressed my worries of the unknowns of marriage and what my past would bring. I was again surprised by God's healing power and on our wedding night and up to date I have not at all been haunted by my past either of sexual abuse or homosexual memories.

The stamp of my healing came almost two years after we were married. It was the birth of our first child, David. It was so significant and special to hold my son after he was born. I realized that this was something the devil had tried to steal, kill and destroy in my life. Since then we have had another son, Hank, and I am currently pregnant with our third child. I have come to recognize that raising godly children is the ultimate treasure. Our kids are the fruit of my wholeness and the evidence of my healing.

Write Your Story

Write Your Story

Perfect People Syndrome

A S WE FACE healing our hurts in this post modern era, we need to discuss one more group, perfect people. Our missional church community in the violent 'hood comprised addicts and survivors of torture, rape, and incest who found wholeness and help. Among the healing folk sat rows of perfect people. They dressed well, exhibited excellent hygiene, and smelled refreshing in the stench of our building. Perfect people carried big Bibles with religious heritage and attended church with hyper vigilance. They stood strong in their beliefs and grinned a lot. They tithed with textbook precision and executed the spiritual life flawlessly.

I meet perfect pastors in coffee shops. They report that their lives, children, and ministries stand faultless, idyllic, like the unspoiled Garden of Eden. And I wonder what went wrong with me. Perfection does not define me . . . I am flawed. I find depth and meaning in what I do, but the church I serve is not the unspoiled Garden. At times it wafts the air of soiled Pampers, not unsullied perfection. The people I hang with do not execute textbook Christianity with precision and neither do I. Over the years I have also discovered that perfect people are the toughest to get along with. They often project a rigid, whiny, difficult, and self-absorbed perfectionism. When I compare my biker addicts and survivors of torture to the perfect people, I would much rather hang out with the former. Scratching your head yet?

Let's examine a perfect person candidate in the life of Christ. A rich young yuppie came to Christ. He started with the warm-up . . . excellent sales tactic. "Good teacher" . . . . Jesus had him at hello. "Why do you call me good?" The yuppie states, "I want to invest in eternal life for a good return on my investment." Jesus says, "You know the commandments." Then the guy interrupts the Son of God.

Let's say you have curable cancer. Halfway through the course of chemotherapy you cut short treatment and pull out the IV. Incredible. The perfect guy interrupts Christ and says, "I have slam-dunked all these commandments since my youth. Check 'em off your palm pilot and give me something difficult to conquer. I have nailed them all" (Luke 18:18-24).

This man was perfect . . . rich . . . clearly confident about himself. Not only well-to-do, he perfectly obeyed the laws of God from childhood. He projected a messianic aura. One barrier in this thinking, no one performs law flawlessly. Impossible.

Anxiety reaction began this man's white knuckle grip on perfect performance and wealth. The rich young yuppie found a sense of soothing and balance when he made big bucks. He paid the bills, felt affirmed, his neurons habituated accustomed to the good feelings associated with making money. He also found affirmation and relief from anxiety when he performed religiously. Neurons have a strong memory about what creates homeostasis. He performs-it feels good. He achieves more. Eventually he needs more performance-oriented behavior to feel the same relief. Shame becomes a wrestling match, however. He knows he cannot perform faultlessly. Imbalance. Anxiety reacts. Neurons adapt and full blown addiction results.

In Mark 10:21 the Scriptures delight in detail, *"Jesus looked at him and loved the man" NIV*. Christ cherished him, and addressed the core of anxiety and addiction. Jesus said, *"Sell your assets and give them to the poor, then you will have treasure in heaven. Then come, follow me."* The perfect guy walks off the basketball court to the locker room. No slam-dunk, no game-winning shot at the buzzer. He feels loss. Multiple systems respond to the anxiety of losing that which created feelings of balance. Withdrawal. He hangs his head, depressed, dejected. Perfect People Syndrome covers for addictive thinking.

Jesus often encountered perfect people. In the Gospel of John Jesus had an escalating conflict with the Pharisees. I define Phariseeism as Perfect People Syndrome. Here are some Scriptural citations and addictive behaviors of perfect people:

John 2:18-demanding; John 5:9-moralistic about healing on the wrong day; John 5:16–persecuted Jesus for healing on the Sabbath. The perfect people denied the validity of Christ's healing ministry due to a rigid interpretation of law; John 6.41-grumbling about His preaching; John 6.52-argumentative; John 7:1-conspiracy to murder Jesus; John 7:20-name-calling; John 7:30-attempted to assault Christ; John 7.32-attempted to arrest Christ; John 8.6-manipulative control; John 8:13-more arguing; John 8:48-name-calling; John 8:52-more name calling; John 8:59-violence; John 9:28-insulting; John 9.34-violence; John 10.31-violence; John 11.37-critical of healing; John 11:53-hierarchical conspiracy to murder-rationalized Jesus' execution as a political necessity; John 12:10-Ibid. Lazarus; John 18:3-violence; John 18.22-violence; John 19.6-violence; John 19:18-the perfect people projected blame and sanctioned the murder of Christ.

The Pharisees memorized Scripture, were textbook devotees to religious ideals, attended worship services, prayed, and tithed. They felt pride over the gifts of law, temple, and sacrifice. Pharisees also committed their lives to executing the legal system flawlessly. And they were often rigid, whiny, difficult, self-absorbed, and the most violent people group in the New Testament. Give me a biker ex felon, or a gun-packing prostitute any day.

I am more Pharisee with Perfect Person Syndrome than I care to admit. Under the right stresses I respond not with faith and reason, but with anger and fear, the fight and flight response of anxiety reaction. I deny control, and rationalize away His power. I stop listening to the speech of God. I also feel chronic anxiety to be accepted and loved by God. Performance-based religion causes my anxiety to diminish. However, when I do not perform flawlessly, I feel greater anxiety. I repeat performance–based religious behaviors to regain balance. Neurons habituate. I need more perfect behaviors for balance. I continue to fall short of religious expectations. Neurotransmitters and receptors release more chemicals in the brain to adjust to greater stress. Neurons adapt unable to tolerate the heightened state of anxiety. Cells change in chemical composition to create the new balance. Full blown addiction results. If I experience failure, imperfect people, or remove my performance-based boundaries, then I feel withdrawal symptoms: I become rigid, whiny, difficult, and self–absorbed filled with guilt and shame. Clinebell states that, "Perfectionism, a prevalent problem in addicted persons, is actually a form of self punishment. Inevitable failures to reach unrealistic goals are followed by self punishing shame and guilt, also common problems among alcoholics and other addicts. An articulate alcoholic wrote in his anonymous autobiography: 'I was crucified on the bitter angle that guilt cuts across the rigid upright of every American's Puritanism.'" (Clinebell, p. 67). Perfect People Syndrome is classic addictive behavior.

Reflect on the people in your life, the religious leader, the CEO, the parent, the spouse. Got flawless folks in your life? Does perfect people syndrome permeate you, punish you? Do you wreak havoc on others who cannot perform?

Linger over these words again, "*Jesus looked and loved . . . you will possess treasure . . . follow me.*" Listen to the one who loves. Track the healer whose hands honed the Himalayas and now tenderly touches your trauma. Look at the adoration in His eyes and the lines of His smile. He cherishes you with every flaw. Drink in His delicate drawl, He invites you to let loose the white knuckle grip on perfection. Step onto the sandy silhouette of Galilean sandals and follow carpenter footprints . . . you belong. One prayer separates you from experiencing the wonder of His love . . . treasure.

Small Group Bible Study

1. Look at these passages again which portray the behavior of the perfect people in the New Testament. What are your reflections? Have you known perfect people? Have you been one?

    Here are some Scriptural citations and addictive behaviors of perfect people:

    John 2:18-demanding; John 5:9-moralistic about healing on the wrong day; John 5:16–persecuted Jesus for healing on the Sabbath. The perfect people denied the validity of Christ's healing ministry due to a rigid interpretation of law; John 6.41-grumbling about His preaching; John 6.52-argumentative; John 7:1-conspiracy to murder Jesus; John 7:20-name-calling; John 7:30-attempted to assault Christ; John 7.32-attempted to arrest Christ; John 8.6-manipulative control; John 8:13-more arguing; John 8:48-name-calling; John 8:52-more name calling; John 8:59-violence; John 9:28-insulting; John 9.34-violence; John 10.31-violence; John 11.37-critical of healing; John 11:53-hierarchical conspiracy to murder-rationalized Jesus' execution as a political necessity; John 12:10-Ibid. Lazarus; John 18:3-violence; John 18.22-violence; John 19.6-violence; John 19:18-the perfect people projected blame and sanctioned the murder of Christ.

2. Although perfect, Jesus has a different attitude. Discuss this statement Jesus made to the Rich Young Yuppie. In Mark 10:21 the Scriptures delight in detail, *"Jesus looked at him and loved the man" NIV.* Christ cherished him. Jesus said, *"Sell your assets and give them to the poor, then you will have treasure in heaven. Then come, follow me."* How is Jesus different than the perfect people?

3. What can you do to release the white knuckle grip of perfection?

4. Several of you read your story. Reflect. Pray together as a group. Be gentle.

Writing Your Story, Healing Your Heart

This piece involves the need to be perfect. Share with your group the anxieties you have had to be perfect. Write your story below. Read Clare's account of her need to be perfect.

Clare's Story

My freshman year in high school I met my first boyfriend, Bill. We fell in love and I spent every hour of my days with him and his family. They owned a gorgeous house in Grand Haven, two cars, a cat and a dog. They didn't have a white picket fence, but they had matching furniture and they bought their food with cash.

My single mom worked hard, but we never seemed to have much to go around. I didn't know the implications this had on our socioeconomic status until I met my boyfriend. I began to unintentionally use his family as the standard that I didn't measure up to.

When I turned 16, I went to work, and got my driver's license. I'd go days without seeing my family except in passing when I crept into my room at 2:00 am. I was always out the door again in the morning by seven, stopping only to pick up the occasional $2 mom would leave for me on the kitchen table for lunch.

On the nights that I had to be home, I fought with my family relentlessly. I knew when to throw the low-blows and what buttons to push to cause the most pain.

When I was a junior in high school, my best friend Laura, began starving herself and was admitted into North Ottawa Hospital for severe anorexia. Her battle continued for a decade, and she was never the same. There was nothing I could do to make her healthy, and I felt so angry at her for leaving me.

When my struggle between what I thought I wanted to be and who I really was got harder to fight, I began to spiral into a suicidal depression. Bill and his family were there for me as I went to psychologists, doctors, and antidepressants.

Once in college, I learned that being on my own brought out the perfectionist in me. I demanded a lot of myself. I had to have a spotless room in immaculate order. I would straighten everything that was already straight every time I entered my room. I would stress out about failing exams so much that I would just procrastinate studying, then ironically fail them. I continued to struggle with depression in college. I'd spend days curled up on my bed under artificial lights. I'd stare numbly at the pebble print carpet, and white cement walls and think. While in this hibernating thought, I'd mainly focus on my family. I still had a lot of childhood anger built up. I felt that my only younger brother didn't like me either, because he was under the impression that I thought I was better than he. Did he know how I spent my days?

Write Your Story of the Need to be Perfect

SECTION TWO

THE BIBLICAL STORY OF
HEALING LIFE'S HURTS

Attachment, Addiction, and Idolatry

ATTACHMENT COMES FROM the French word, *attaché*, which means "nailed to". Attachment drives a nail through our thoughts and emotions into objects, people, or actions. So close to the object we cannot see our attachment to it. The paradox of being attached to anything but loving God is that addiction and idolatry thrive on the energy to control it (May, p. 4).

> The longer an addiction continues, the more things will become associated with it and the more entrenched it will become . . . The longer it lasts the more powerful it becomes. Attachments are thus like spreading malignancies, steadily invading and incorporating their surroundings into themselves. To apply the words of Isaiah, addictions are like "greedy dogs, never satisfied", or as Habakkuk said, "Forever on the move, with an appetite as large as sheol, and as insatiable as death" (May, p. 86).

Attachment acts like a spiritual Ebola devouring life energy through obsessions and compulsions, resulting in loss of energy to love. A spiritual writer has called it, a "counterfeit of religious presence" (May, p. 13). Perfect People Syndrome is this . . . a fabricated presence forged in the anxiety of being imperfect, shamed, and rejected. In this section I will point out the connections between idolatry, attachment, and addiction. Idolatry-attachment happens in a three step process: 1) Feeling of gratification or relief from anxiety attached to an activity or object; 2)

Repeating the activity to again feel pleasure or relief; 3) Loss of restraint or control (May, pp. 57-60).

There are five characteristics of idolatry-attachment-addiction:1) tolerance—wanting or needing more. Satiation seems ridiculous. 2) withdrawal symptoms—anxiety arises when the body senses deprivation of the attachment. Danger signals result; i.e. uneasy, irritable, anxious, and panicky behaviors. Backlash takes place when cellular balancing systems rebound or swing in opposite directions. Withdrawal from ethyl alcohol can make the lethargic become hyperactive, and withdrawal from stimulants can produce depressive behaviors. If perfection is my addiction, I become anxious and irritable when imperfection presents; 3) self-deception keeps an attachment behavior going; 4) loss of willpower-one part of us wants to be free, another wants to continue the feelings of attachment that are much stronger than the will to be free; 5) distortion of attention-for love to be known, attention must be free to focus. Attachments cover our freedom in preoccupation. We cannot know love because we nail ourselves to an idol-addiction (May, pp. 26-29).

Attachments make up a continuum. On one end visualize attachments or idols of attraction and on the other, aversion. Attachments of attraction are things, people, thinking which draw us. Our mind and body feel pleasure or relief from anxiety and ultimately need more of the attachment to feel the same relief. Attachments of aversion are things, people, and thinking which repel us. However, the revulsion brings a strange sense of soothing.

Idolatry becomes any attachment that eclipses our relationship with God. One of the most impacting small group Bible studies I have ever been involved with examined idolatry and grace in Isaiah. One of the teaching tools we used involved giving a list of attachments to the participants. The response to this method evoked awe, anger, frustration, grief, and thankfulness for the uncovering of addictive idolatrous behavior. I will cite the same lists for effect. The following catalogs idols of attraction. Each item by itself may not be dangerous, but when we become nailed to it, then the process of detachment from God begins. Here is a list of idols of attraction:

> anger, approval, art, attractiveness, being-good, helpful, loved, nice, right, taken care of; calendars, candy, cars, cats, causes, chewing gum, children, chocolate, cleanliness, coffee, comparisons, competence, competition, computers, contests, death, depression, dreams, drinking, drugs, eating, envy, exercise, fame, family, fantasies, finger drumming, fishing, food, friends, furniture, gambling, gardening, golf, gossiping, groups, guilt, hair twisting, happiness, hobbies, housekeeping, humor, hunting, ice cream, images of God, intimacy, jealousy, knowledge, lying, marriage, meeting expectations, memories, messiness, money, movies, music, nail biting, neatness, parents, performance, pets, pimple squeezing, pistachio nuts,

pizza, politics, popcorn, popularity, potato chips, power, psychotherapy, punctuality, reading, relationships, responsibility, revenge, scab picking, seductiveness, self image, self improvement, sex, shoplifting, sleeping, soft drinks, sports, status, stock market, stress, sunbathing, suspiciousness, talking, television, time, tobacco, weight, winning, work, worthiness (May, p. 38).

Some things to which we attach bring relief from anxiety, but at the same time they repulse. Here is an inventory of idols of aversion:

airplanes, anchovies, anger, animals, being-abnormal, alone, discounted, fat, judged, overwhelmed, thin, tricked: birds, blood, boredom, bridges, bugs, cats, closed in spaces, commitment, conflict, crowds, darkness, death, dentists, dependence, dirt, disapproval, doctors, embarrassment, evil spirits, failure, fire, germs, guilt, high places, illness, independence, intimacy, mice, needles, open spaces, pain, people of different-beliefs, class, culture, politics, race, religion, sex; People who are-addicted, competent, fat, thin, ignorant, neat, messy, rich, poor: public speaking, rats, rejection, responsibility, sex, sharp instruments, slimy creatures, snakes, spiders, storms, strangers, success, tests, traffic, tunnels, vulnerability, water, writing (May, p. 39).

Addictive behavior manifests what we in the Christian community call idolatry. It is any attachment that eclipses compassion for and loyalty to God. An attachment becomes a barrier to loving, caring for and being faithful in relationship. Paul Tillich said that our God is whatever we are ultimately concerned with (May, p. 29). When we review the five characteristics of attachment-addiction: 1) tolerance; 2) withdrawal; 3) self deception; 4) loss of willpower; 5) distortion of attention; we see that all five characterize idolatry in the Bible.

The book of Isaiah represents the ministry of this prophet beginning during the crises around the attack on Jerusalem in 732 B.C. He points out how the people attach themselves to elaborate rituals and eventually to extravagant celebrations worshiping other gods. In other words his prophecies chart the people taking steps toward idolatry. In this he touches on the five characteristics of attachment-addiction: 1) tolerance–wanting or needing more. There is never enough of the attachment. *"The idols of Babylon, Bel and Nebo, are being hauled away on carts"* Isaiah 46:1 NIV. *"Call out the demon hordes you have worshiped all these years"* Isaiah 47:12 NIV; 2) withdrawal symptoms – *"GOD spoke strongly to me, grabbed me with both hands and warned me not to go along with this people. He said: 'Don't be like this people, always afraid somebody is plotting against them. Don't fear what they fear. Don't take on their worries. If you're going to worry, worry about The Holy'"* Isaiah 8.11-13MSG. Anxiety reacts resulting in worry and fear when deprived of the attachment; 3) self deception is the exquisite ingenuity of the mind to keep an attachment behavior going. *"They carry it (idol) on their shoulders, and when they set it down, it stays there. It cannot move. And when someone prays to it there is no answer. It has no power to get anyone out of trouble"* Isaiah 46:7 NIV; 4) loss of willpower—one part of us wants to be free. Another wants to continue the much stronger feelings of attachment. *"You are a pleasure crazy kingdom, living at ease and feeling secure, bragging as if you were the greatest in the world. You say, 'I'm self sufficient and not accountable to anyone. I will never be a widow or lose my children'"* Isaiah 47:8 NIV; 5) distortion of attention—for love to be known, attention must focus freely. Attachments cover our freedom in preoccupation. We cannot know love because we are nailed to an idol-addiction. *"You did not care at all about my people or think about the consequences of your actions"* Isaiah 47:7 NIV (May, pp. 26-29).

Isaiah exposes the idolatry of the people, but he also talks about grace overcoming the grip of idolatry. In Isaiah 2 grace presents as a place of kingdom community, Jerusalem. In chapter 11 grace personifies as a person of Davidic descent, foreshadowing Jesus Christ. In chapter 35 grace becomes a pathway to Jerusalem, from exile and brokenness to wholeness.

Isaiah 2 begins with a focus on Jerusalem, God's mountain, the location of His presence and grace-filled community. *"In the last days the mountain of the Lord's temple will be established as chief among the mountains; it will be raised above the hills and all nations will stream to it"* Isaiah 2:2 NIV. Following are some descriptors of Jerusalem. At this location God will: teach us his ways so we may walk in his paths, send out his law from this location and he will speak (3). He will judge nations; the result will be peace (4). At this geographical location God shows how he will relate to humanity. At this locale the people of Israel are challenged to walk in the light of the Lord (5) and cease trusting in man (22). Isaiah also describes the barriers to experiencing grace. He uses deep sensational language. The emotion most penetrating and painful for God is . . . abandonment. *"You have abandoned your people* (6)."

I have counseled hundreds of addicts over thousands of hours. One of the top painful events in life is abandonment. When a parent, a spouse, or a lover leaves, the pain pierces deep launching anxiety reaction and addictive behavior. I have led numerous twelve-step groups. Every addict in the circle had a parent who abandoned whether through death, addiction, or abuse. When we leave God, he hurts the deepest.

Abandonment takes on particular shapes. They are: materialism: *"Their land is full of silver and gold; there is no end to their treasures* (7)"; and attachment to idols: *"Their land is full of idols; they bow down to the work of their hands, to what their fingers have made* (8)."

Note that God's locale is defined by teaching His way of grace, law, justice, and peace. Attachments define the Israelis' geography. The driving emotion behind this abandonment . . . pride, *"The eyes of the arrogant man will be humbled and the pride of men brought low . . . . (11)* " Consequences happen to the kind of pride that caused the abandonment, *"The arrogance of man will be brought low and the pride of men humbled . . . the idols will totally disappear (17)".*

God created a striking place to empower His community of faith, Jerusalem. He chiseled the image of His grace in stone, concrete, not ethereal. Purity and loveliness of the topography reflect God's heart for His people. Jerusalem geographically is stunning. Grace defines as beauty. Jerusalem sets high on a mountain and looks over the pastoral lands of Judah. Grace stoops to embrace. The Israelites built Jerusalem as a mighty fortress. Grace is the most powerful word for love in the Old Testament. Grace flows through reciprocity of relationship. Jerusalem has gates through which the worshiper enters by his choice. The writers of Scripture portray an indestructibility of Zion. Grace stands as sovereign decree. Jerusalem means city of peace. Grace is covenant and results in peace for the parties who enter into relationship. Jerusalem creates safety for its inhabitants; it outlines the locale of forgiveness, mercy, and presence of God. Grace frames our salvation and embodies the same elements of forgiveness, mercy, and presence (Botterweck, pp. 22-36). Jerusalem paints one of the most beautiful treasure themes in the Bible. The Book of Revelation reaffirms this image. God recreates New Jerusalem in the final scene, the climax. Look at the plethora of treasure images.

I saw the Holy City, New Jerusalem, coming down out of heaven from God prepared as a bride beautifully dressed for her husband . . . and its brilliance was like that of a very precious jewel, like a jasper, clear as crystal.
Revelation 21. 2 and 21.10-11 NIV

Chapter 11 describes the relationship of grace in terms of a person, a descendant of King David. This person will be characterized by: the Spirit of wisdom, understanding, counsel, power, knowledge, and of deep reverence for God (2). He will be an advocate for the poor, righteous and faithful (5). There will be peace under his leadership (6). The nations will come to him (10). He will gather exiles and restore them to the place of grace (11). This is God's passion–that exiled Israel will return to His place to experience grace. A person from the royal family of David, Jesus Christ, paves the way for this homecoming.

Grace is not an impersonal force or new age energy. Chapter 11 paints the picture of a person who embodies and dispenses grace. Grace loves the lesser. The Davidic leader cares for the poor. Grace overcomes sin. This person defeats division. Grace brings adverse parties together. This individual reconciles antagonistic nations. In these two chapters Isaiah shows the concrete nature of God's grace geographically and personally. The character traits of this person embody an empathic spirit and an intimacy with God climaxed by deep revering. The word hinging these concepts . . . power. Jerusalem is a power plant of grace. This descendant of David presents a dynamic force. Parallels to grace are righteousness and faithfulness. The person is both righteous and faithful. Grace belongs to the realm of community, the deepest of loves which bind peoples together. Grace embodied will bring an exiled community back to the place of grace. God wants His people within the power plant and he will utilize a person to do so. Grace is about community, a city, a people impacted by a person, a disenfranchised nation recovering from exile and brokenness being made whole within a powerful locale (Botterweck, pp. 22-36).

Chapter 35 expresses grace in terms of pathway from the brokenness of exile to wholeness. The operative passage is, *"A highway shall be there and a pathway, and it shall be called the way of holiness . . . the redeemed shall walk there. And the ransomed of the Lord shall return and come to Zion with songs and everlasting joy upon their heads; they shall obtain joy and gladness, and sorrow and sighing shall flee away"* Isaiah 35.8-10 *KJV.* Chapter 35 begins and ends with gladness, rejoicing. The chapter climaxes when the community of Israel returns to God's power plant of grace, Jerusalem.

The descriptors of the path in chapter 35 are: the glory and excellence of God (2); the wholeness of man in which: fearful become strong (4); the eyes of the blind open and the deaf hear (5); and the lame not only walk, but they leap skillfully (6). Healing extends also to the natural order: the wilderness blossoms and arid regions flourish (1,6). The human spirit heals next: the way will be holiness, purity of relationship with God and the unclean will not pass through (8); the whole will walk in safety (9); the exiles will return to Jerusalem ransomed by God and the place of His grace and power is made complete (10).

Isaiah begins with the place and ends with pathway to this locale. The central figure is the Davidic person. Grace like a power plant transforms idolatrous addicted hearts through community, Davidic descendent, and the pathway of brokenness. The grace of God brings wholeness to heartbreak. The Book of Revelation like a bookend tells the same story. In chapter 21 you see the lamb on the throne and the faith community gathered worshiping Him within the walls of New Jerusalem surrounded by stunning beauty. The broken places of their lives are healed and touched by the powerful presence of Christ. This scene shines with treasure for the human heart.

Now the dwelling of God is with men and He will live with them. They will be His people and God Himself will be with them and be their God. He will wipe every tear from their eyes. There will be no more death or mourning or crying or pain for the old order of things has passed away.
Vss. 3-4

He who was seated on the throne said, "I am making everything new."
Vs. 5

The nations will walk by its light and the kings of the earth will bring their splendor into it. Vs. 24

The treasure in Isaiah and Revelation unearths as a city and a Savior for a society of healing people. Jesus Christ leads the banished to this place of belonging. Filled with grace he is wise, understanding, and guides with truth and integrity. He gathers the broken-hearted in His arms like a shepherd embraces his lambs. He leads them from the exile of attachments, idolatry, and addiction on a roadway paved with their own brokenness to a place of powerful community. He beautifies this place and people with sapphire, emeralds, topaz, amethyst, pearls, and pure gold. God loves His treasure and uses the most powerful words in literature to describe His passion. This is God's grace for addicted, traumatized, and perfect people. Here you will find His tender touch to wipe your tears.

Small Group Bible Study

1. Look at this passage of Scripture from Habakkuk. What does this tell you about attachments, addiction, sin?

    > *"Furthermore, wine betrays the haughty man,*
    > *So that he does not stay at home*
    > *He enlarges his appetite like Sheol,*
    > *And he is like death, never satisfied.*
    > *Habakkuk 2:5 (New American Standard Bible)*

2. The book of Revelation paints a beautiful picture of what healing for your heart looks like. Read chapters 21 and 22 together from several different translations and discuss the power of this scene to heal your life.

    > *Now the dwelling of God is with men and he will live with them. They will be His people and God Himself will be with them and be their God. He will wipe every tear from their eyes. There will be no more death or mourning or crying or pain for the old order of things has passed away.Vss. 3-4 He who was seated on the throne said, "I am making everything new." Vs. 5 The nations will walk by its light and the kings of the earth will bring their splendor into it.*
    > *Vs. 24*

3. How is Jesus making you new?

4. Power exists in the presence of God. Nothing outshines the light of God . . . nothing. What barriers stand between you and the Lord?

Beth's Story

I remember the first moment I started cutting.

I was sitting on the sofa in the living room. My husband was sitting at the other end engrossed in a TV show. Inside I felt so overwhelmed with emotional pain I felt as if my life would end if I did not do something.

The thought of cutting had not entered my mind until I'd read about it in a book. It made sense: cutting to relieve emotional pain and anguish.

Why I selected that day and time I don't know. Perhaps my husband being there was significant – an internal cry for help – hoping he would see the depth of my pain and respond to me in a more caring and present way.

Instead he reacted. Disgusted. With repulsion. Telling me in no uncertain terms that I was worse than he thought. Then he left. It was what he always did. And I was alone again, filled with more shame piled on top of the already overwhelming pain inside. So I cut to punish myself for the badness that was me.

I also remember the last time I cut.

My husband and I were separated and I was living in a 1-room apartment, standing in front of the mirror, looking at myself wishing the pain would go away. I picked up a razor blade and started making a careful incision in my arm. As I waited for the blood to start coming, I heard a voice inside my head, different from any other voice to that moment. It said "you don't have to bleed, I already did. For you."

A tidal wave of warm peace overflowed my entire being and I put down the razor and wept.

Jesus was present. He knew about the cutting I'd been doing for the past few years. He had watched me, felt my pain and all the helplessness that went with it. He knew I wanted to give up on life, and He also knew that in some small part of my being I hoped there was a reason not to. He chose that moment to say something profound, in a context that was significant, in words that went far below the surface cuts and deep into my heart of hearts.

I never cut after that.

Sometimes the temptation was there, but His words resonated so deeply the enticement was diffused.

It's been 14 years since I picked up a razor or scissors to cut myself. After that day in my bathroom I continued to work through the recovery of years of just about every type of trauma you can imagine. The divorce was final, I went back to school and completed my Master's degree, and now work as a counselor helping people heal from deep hurts.

It's still difficult for me to put myself in the shoes of the caregiver of someone who cuts. I understand so well the depth of pain and shame and the nonsensical sense it makes to self-mutilate. I find myself amazed at the negative reactions of parents, spouses, friends, pastors, even counselors, toward those who cut.

The Bible talks about self-mutilation, and most significant to me is the story in Mark chapter 5. Jesus had been enjoying the people, teaching them parables about the Kingdom of God and spending time with his disciples. That night they got into a boat to go across the lake to find a self-mutilator and heal him. But his disciples didn't know that yet. Interesting that this trip was also the one where they got to know the Lord and the extent of his power over nature, calming the "furious squall" (NIV) which would surely have taken their lives if not for his authority.

> *He got up, rebuked the wind and said to the waves, "Quiet! Be still!" Then the wind died down and it was completely calm. He said to his disciples, "Why are you so afraid? Do you still have no faith?" They were terrified and asked each other, "Who is this? Even the wind and the waves obey him!"*
> *(Mark 5:39-41)*

I find it interesting that Jesus took this specific opportunity to challenge their faith and their fears. Perhaps because of what was coming next. He was teaching them to trust him, that he had all authority over everything helpless, and that no matter what was happening around them there was no need to fear.

I find in my own life experience with cutting, as well as the times I've talked with those who cut and those who care for cutters, that there is a lot of fear. Certainly my husband responded out of fear. Fear I would really hurt myself. Fear he would come home and find me covered in blood. Fear I would take my life. He would take all the knives and scissors and razors in the house and hide them because of fear. Withdrawing more was also because of fear. He did not know what would happen and was doing his best to protect me. At the same time he was afraid of if/when/how things might escalate and didn't know how to deal with it so he left.

Self-mutilation is an extreme response to suffering. It is also completely dark and demonic. I truly believe that if Satan can get someone to start cutting or engaging in other self-harm activities, he feels a certain level of triumph and the victim feels an increasing sense of helplessness and aloneness which takes them farther and farther into the darkness and deeper into cutting.

Jesus used a fierce storm to make a statement to his disciples that he had authority over the darkness, and was not afraid to engage it, nor would he leave someone when the storm was raging.

The other thing about this passage which stands out is that Jesus intentionally went to the other side of the lake. What was there? A huge crowd of fans awaiting the arrival of the Messiah and his rock band of disciples? A mega-church that had promoted a Jesus concert as a way of evangelizing their city? Perhaps a resort with all the amenities for him and his disciples to enjoy a relaxing vacation before they started back on the Jerusalem Road?

None of these things were waiting for Christ. In fact, reading Mark 5 it could be inferred that this area was filled with darkness to the point that after Christ's work was done the people begged him to leave. They wanted nothing of Him and His power and love and healing.

What *was* waiting for Jesus was a deeply troubled young man, who was so intensely afflicted by a legion of demons that he lived among the tombs continuously cutting himself with stones.

I don't know his history. I do know that most people who self-mutilate have abuse in their background and the enemy has used these violations to take them into dark places of self-harm.

What is significant is that Jesus sought this man out. He left crowds on the other shore, traveled by boat overnight, through an intense storm, to find this one individual who was hurting. And he took authority and set him free from the destructive attacks of the enemy.

I love that he included this story in the written Gospels. Jesus was not afraid of shame and pain. He pursued the one who was overwhelmed and overcome by it and did not shun him. He reached out to him – one of the few times he did that. Usually he waited for people to seek him out. But he knew this man was not able to do that – he was drowning in a dark pit and needed the Savior to come to him. That is love – such a stark contrast to the hatred that motivates abuse and the shame that drives self-mutilation.

When someone hurts themselves they don't understand love – it's something they long for but not something they believe in. They've lost hope for love because what was presented as love only hurt. Truth is skewed to the point of believing they only deserve hurt. And whether it's inflicted on them by someone else or not, they receive it, welcoming it, even, as earned and justified.

It takes time to heal from hurt like that. It takes people who believe in the one who lives in this depth of dark – believe they are loveable, they are loved, and they deserve to be loved. It takes consistent, patient acceptance from someone who loves like Jesus.

Almost a year ago I saw an ad for an organization that reaches out to hurting people – it's called TWLOHA (To Write Love On Her Arms) and they promote healing deeper pain that is behind self-mutilation. They aren't a Christian organization, but their premise certainly has the love of Christ written in it. I've lived with scars on my arms which never go away. Something struck me when I read about TWLOHA and I wondered what my arms would look like if "Love" could be written on them – permanently. I decided to have a special tattoo created by a friend, one that says "Love" in beautiful script, and is written over the scars. The scars are still there, but barely visible because when I (or anyone else) look at my arm now, "Love" is written there, and I remember that I am lovable, I am loved, and I deserve love.

That is the Savior's message to you, to me, to everyone in this world – and it's why He came, to prove the reality of Love.

Something else I've learned since getting the tattoo – He's got a tattoo also. Written in the palms of His hands are the pictures of His kids. He never forgets us, He never loses sight of the hurt. The context of that truth in Isaiah involves a mother's wounding toward her child–abandonment. Here's how the Amplified Bible writes it:

"[And the Lord answered] Can a woman forget her nursing child, that she should not have compassion on the son of her womb? Yes, they may forget, yet I will not forget you. Behold, I have indelibly imprinted (tattooed a picture of) you on the palm of each of My hands."

Isaiah 49:15-16

There is no pain that His hands won't heal. There is no wound His eyes will ever turn away from. There is no one whom He will not embrace with joyous and profound Love.

The next time you hurt to the point of hurting yourself, pause for a moment, listen for His voice whispering His love for you. You don't have to hurt yourself any more. He hurt for you. You are lovable. You are worth loving. And you are loved.

Writing Your Story, Healing Your Heart

This is a fun one. Look at the list of attachments and share with your group which ones you excel at. Circle the ones you think you have. If you are brutally honest, ask your good friends which ones you possess. Have any attachments become idols? Talk about this. Write out your story of attachments below. Here is a list of idols of attraction:

> anger, approval, art, attractiveness, being-good, helpful, loved, nice, right, taken care of; calendars, candy, cars, cats, causes, chewing gum, children, chocolate, cleanliness, coffee, comparisons, competence, competition, computers, contests, death, depression, dreams, drinking, drugs, eating, envy, exercise, fame, family, fantasies, finger drumming, fishing, food, friends, furniture, gambling, gardening, golf, gossiping, groups, guilt, hair twisting, happiness, hobbies, housekeeping, humor, hunting, ice cream, images of God, intimacy, jealousy, knowledge, lying, marriage, meeting expectations, memories, messiness, money, movies, music, nail biting, neatness, parents, performance, pets, pimple squeezing, pistachio nuts, pizza, politics, popcorn, popularity, potato chips, power, psychotherapy, punctuality, reading, relationships, responsibility, revenge, scab picking, seductiveness, self image, self improvement, sex, shoplifting, sleeping, soft drinks, sports, status, stock market, stress, sunbathing, suspiciousness, talking, television, time, tobacco, weight, winning, work, worthiness (May, p. 38).

Some things to which we attach bring relief from anxiety, but at the same time they repulse. Here is an inventory of idols of aversion:

> airplanes, anchovies, anger, animals, being-abnormal, alone, discounted, fat, judged, overwhelmed, thin, tricked: birds, blood, boredom, bridges, bugs, cats, closed in spaces, commitment, conflict, crowds, darkness, death, dentists, dependence, dirt, disapproval, doctors, embarrassment, evil spirits, failure, fire, germs, guilt, high places, illness, independence, intimacy, mice, needles, open spaces, pain, people of different-beliefs, class, culture, politics, race, religion, sex; People who are-addicted, competent, fat, thin, ignorant, neat, messy, rich, poor: public speaking, rats, rejection, responsibility, sex, sharp instruments, slimy creatures, snakes, spiders, storms, strangers, success, tests, traffic, tunnels, vulnerability, water, writing (May, p. 39).

Write Out Your Story of Attachments of Attraction

Write Out Your Story of Attachments of Aversion

The Power of Brokenness

MY BIRTHDAY IS December 26 . . . every year. I hold childhood memories of birthday gifts wrapped in Santa paper. It's difficult competing with the King of kings for birthday favors. Every Christmas baby reading this knows what I mean. Well-meaning family members squeeze the joy of your birth into a hectic and at times impossible holiday schedule. Poor me.

One birthday another awkward gift unwrapped, a Tsunami. In the early hours of December 26, 2004 the deadliest earthquake and Tsunami in five centuries wreaked havoc on the peoples of Indonesia, wiping out coastline villages and over 275,000 lives. A Tsunami begins deep within the ocean floor. Tectonic plates shift. Displacement. The shock sends out a wave of water in all directions the height of a small child. This small swell traveling the speed of a jet is almost undetectable to a boat on the ocean until it assaults land, building a mountainous wall of water 50 feet high. A Tsunami begins deep, silent, and unseen, but its aftermath overwhelms.

Our church planted in a violent neighborhood. The members, attendees, and visitors were predominantly post modern addicts and survivors of trauma. As the only staff member, for some reason I always felt exhausted. In the early days of the church I worked full time in a factory, third shift, scraping paint. Clocking out at 7 a.m., I went to graduate school until 3 p.m. I preached on Wednesdays and Sundays, led four small groups at once, counseled traumatized lives for hundreds of hours a year, managed two boards, mowed the church lawn, cleaned horrible bathrooms, remodeled the auditorium, vacuumed a sea of red carpet, arrived early Sunday mornings so our artists wouldn't kill each other, shoveled snow before church services, and received at times 10 or more counseling phone calls on my day off.

In honest moments I noticed that I was often rigid, whiny, difficult, and self-absorbed. I could not figure out why. I prayed more. Read more Scripture. Served God harder. Implemented more church growth strategies. I recall asking one of my mega coaches about church growth. He sent me a note challenging me to execute one of his seven steps to success. I re-examined my spiritual game and attended more mega church seminars. The hurt went deeper. My wife looked traumatized and my children acted out their disapproval.

I recall a counseling appointment in the 'hood . . . another alcoholic. This day differed, my life changed. I gave him the standard three point sermonic strategy for overcoming addiction. He left. The wave hit.

The alcoholic spent the hour telling me of his rigid, whiny, difficult, and self-absorbed life. Though exhausted, angry, and depressed, he could not stop working, his relationships . . . dying. The Tsunami smashed me in the face at the speed of a jet plane.

Devastated and exposed I own that man's story. Although I don't drink, and am arrogant about it, I have the same exact behaviors.

I call this Spiritual Tsunami. It begins deep within the human spirit building almost without detection. Watch the tectonic plates shift and the wave swell: shame-based workaholism driven by guilt, depressive, irritable, perfectionistic. Focus on rejection because life revolves around me. I won't stop working, can't sit down, always laboring, planning, scheming. I work to the exclusion of my wife, children, and God. I can no longer listen . . . I have the same behaviors as the guy who slams dunks a fifth of Jack Daniels. The wave strikes . . . recedes. I feel broken. Then, this passage.

> *But this precious treasure-this light and power that now shine within us-is held in perishable containers, that is in our weak bodies. So everyone can see that our glorious power is from God and is not our own. We are pressed on every side by troubles, but we are not crushed and broken. We are perplexed but we don't give up and quit. We are hunted down but God never abandons us. We get knocked down but we get up again and keep going.*
> *2 Corinthians 4:7-9 NLT*

In the spiritual journey a precious treasures unearths . . . light and power within our weakness. The result . . . power generates not from us, but from God. We go through hell, washed up, overwhelmed, but God recreates to bring healing and growth in our brokenness.

I began to teach about the goodness of God in my weaknesses. I told the entire church my addictive drug of choice was work with alcoholic attitude shooters. In every small group I opened up about my pain and failure. I sought their accountability and prayer. I slowed down. I listened more . . . talked less. My wife began to like me again. This facet of wholeness uncovers a deeper richness—brokenness.

I believe the power of the church of Jesus Christ is not our strength or gifts, but the presence of God in our weakness. I have friends who edit media for world famous Christian leaders. My production buddies use words like primadonna and abusive. I wonder if my favorite leadership models operate from giftedness rather than brokenness. Spiritual gifts focus on the power of the individual. Brokenness opens doors for the power of God in the weaknesses of the individual. I went to a mega-church leaders' conference, interested in improving my church growth game. The coach, ticked, rigid, whiny, difficult, and self-absorbed, railed at preachers of small churches for not having the right stuff for teaching. I sit with talented and intelligent, philosophical yet rage filled post moderns throwing stones at the treasure of God's heart . . . the church. Giftedness . . . not brokenness.

Think about Jesus . . . the suffering servant. He dies on the cross, vulnerable, transparent, broken. Paul the Apostle spoke openly about his failures and weaknesses. In Romans 7 Paul's autobiography sounds like one of my friends in 12 step recovery. He was beaten, shipwrecked, betrayed, snake bit, imprisoned, abandoned by friends and continents. But the joy, the delight, the power. Paul found treasure chained to a third world prison. Our Barney purple church of addicts and survivors found richness in a war zone. This wealth is neither about giftedness nor abilities, but rather wholeness for addiction and trauma; our weaknesses witness the wonder of God declaring his grace and power.

Spiritual gifts, their discovery and implementation in the church, find biblical support. But a deeper way than giftedness uncovers in the church. The under-the-radar richness is God's power in weakness. My parents divorced by my sixteenth birthday. I now have profound passion for families and marriage. A counselor colleague experienced abuse as a child. This counselor has committed his life to helping children. One of my friends lived a promiscuous lifestyle. He now leads groups of young men on the topic of sexual purity. Another leader in our recovery ministry has had a lifetime attachment to drugs. He helps others recover.

Brokenness, not giftedness, unlocks the door to the transforming Gospel story. What is the broken place in your life? Divorce? Depression? Serve God in the area of your weakness. You will find power there. In the eighties two famous televangelists fell from grace. Each was gifted, powerful. One had a broken marriage. The other suffered a prostitute addiction. The collapse came in part because they ignored the broken places. Don't deny the frailty, embrace God in it. Love children, protect them, hold in high value marriage and singleness. Do you wrestle with porn? Talk to trusted friends. Help other male friends with the same attachment. Serve from brokenness. Giftedness can contribute to denial burying the very truth with which God intends to transform your heart.

Brokenness leads to deeper spirituality and the ability to listen to God. When life is about me and for me, I get by on my gifts and abilities, not God's power. Let me show you a biblical example of gifts and the power of brokenness.

King David's resume resounds as the most gifted leader in the ancient near east. Through his leadership, initiative, and calling, the people of Israel achieved heights of wealth and conquests they had never known. David possessed supreme leadership skills, an artist, a poet, a musician, and a man who loved God deeply. These passages of scripture will give you deeper insight into his character.

> *"I love you lord. You are my strength. The lord is my rock, my fortress and my savior. My God is my rock in whom I find protection. He is my shield, the strength of my salvation and my stronghold. I will call on the Lord who is worthy of praise for He saved me from my enemies. The ropes of death surrounded me, the floods of destruction swept over me, the grave wrapped its ropes around me, and death itself stared me in the face. But in my distress I cried out to the lord. Yes, I prayed to my God for help. He heard me from His sanctuary, my cry reached His ears"*
> *Psalm 18:1-6 NIV.*

David's relationship with God touched titanic proportions. Reflective in his lyrics one can unearth a deep, loving, abiding sensitivity toward the living God. Scripture characterizes David as a man after God's own heart (1 Samuel 13.14).

When David was a young man, the Palestinians and the Israelis fought ferociously. Sound contemporary? These familial enemies stood at a strategic battlefield impasse. One of the elite Special-Force Palestinians stepped out of his ranks and said, "I'll tell you what, send one of your best to fight me. Winner takes all and we will end this thing right now." His name in the Hebrew language is "Golyath". He stood taller than Shaquille O'Neil (1 Samuel 17:10). The Israelis had no Delta Force or SEALs to match this monster. David worked as a shepherd boy, filled with love and integrity for God. David rushes to the front, selects several smooth riverbed stones, and then makes this statement to the big man wearing size 23 EEE sandals: *"You come to me with swords, spear and javelin, but I come to you in the name of the Lord almighty, the God of the armies of Israel whom you have defied. Today, the Lord will conquer you" 1 Samuel 17.45-46 NIV.* Okay, get this guy. David weighs 120 pounds soaking wet and he takes on Shaq in a game of one on one. Standing eyeball to navel David declares, *"Today the Lord will conquer you and everyone will know the fear of the God of Israel. Everyone will know that the Lord does not need weapons to rescue His people. It is His battle, it is not ours, the Lord is going to give you to us" 1 Samuel 17:46 NIV.* David loads his sling and nails the franchise fighter between the eyes. Israel wins. David promotes through the ranks. The king gives his daughter to David in marriage, making him an heir to the throne. David achieves rock star status; incredible gifts, good looking, married to the boss' daughter. Everything seems to go David's way in part because of his giftedness.

A strange phenomenon can take place within gifted people. Under the right kind of anxiety focus shifts. The phenomenon is called thought distortion. Before we take a look at the nuts and bolts of thought distortion, let's look at the results in David's life.

Divorce, tabloid fodder, political intrigue. The historical record states that at the time of year when kings routinely go to war, David didn't. One evening when he walked on the flat roof of the palace high above the other houses in Jerusalem, he saw a woman bathing. As she worshiped through this ceremonial ritual cleansing bath, David lusted her. Because he was the boss and gifted, David didn't ask, he told. She became his lover and conceived. When he found out about the baby, David conspired to legitimize the affair by murdering her husband. To cover that crime he allowed a whole division of the army to die also (2 Samuel 11:1-6).

How could a man so gifted, so close to God, crash and burn? When anxiety presents, thinking processes alter. This is called thought distortion (Twerski, p. 41). The first twist in thinking is denial, "I don't have a problem, really I'm fine." The second subtle distortion rationalizes, "If I did do it, it is ok. Valid reasons drove my choices." The third facet of thought distortion projects, "Not only do I not have any issues, you are my problem." Ever caught one of your kids in the cookie jar? From the furthest corner of the house, you hear the clanking of the lid. You accuse the culprit, "Johnny, did you eat a cookie?" His mouth bulges looking like a chipmunk with chocolate chips hanging from his quivering chin. You confront, he denies. I try not to pick on our politicians, but the illustrative material excels. Do you recall one of our former politicians and his oval office affair? "I did not have sexual relations with that woman!" Remember the finger pointing, "I did not!"? Denial. Then rationalization, parsing the word "is". Finally he projected the blame and the political turmoil for his affair on right wing conspiracies. Thought distortion (Twerski, p. 41).

Denial, rationalization and projection happen unconsciously. When a physical injury causes imbalance, white blood cells multiply rapidly in bone marrow and move directly to the source of injury, coagulants and platelets appear to stop the bleeding. Antitoxins form to help stop other foreign bodies from entering our blood stream. All of this happens unawares to protect the body. Our brain engages unconscious processes to establish a new homeostasis. Thought distortion enters to bring harmony to multiple systems of anxious neurons. When thought distortion reacts, reality becomes elusive. It's like asking a blind person to describe the color purple. Distortion of thought can neither perceive behavior nor form appropriate questions to ask. The addict may be far from reality, but believes every word he says (Twerski, pp. 41-42).

David commits an affair and orders mass murder. The distortion of thought had become so deep that he couldn't perceive the condition of his own heart. David lived the lie until confronted and broken. Look at the entry point of wholeness for this great man in Psalm 51: *"Have mercy on me oh God according to your unfailing love. According to your great compassion, blot out my transgressions" NIV.* David could not listen until brokenness brought him to the bottom. Look at the words. Have mercy on me. Unfailing love. Great compassion. His brokenness opened the door to God's power. David's covenantal words express the deepest love and loyalty possible. David's brokenness defines a transformational moment in his life. David sins, the Tsunami strikes, and he feels his shame. Then David goes deeper, *"Create in me a pure heart, oh God, and renew a steadfast spirit within me. Don't cast me from your presence or take your Holy Spirit from me. Restore to me the joy of your salvation. Grant for me a willing spirit to sustain me" Psalm 51:10 NIV.* A spiritual Tsunami breaks the great leader. Deeper relationship results not based on his gifts or performance, but on the love and grace of God. David made monumental mistakes. His thinking at times was nuts, but his family produced the treasure, Jesus Christ. Brokenness opens the door to power.

Every wonder what it will take to grow deeper spiritually? Is the answer working harder, praying more, checking off strategic lists and purpose statements? Or perhaps a richer spirituality engages a different entry point. Vacation. Upper Peninsula, Michigan. Lori, the kids and I rest for a couple of weeks traveling through beautiful country of crystal clear lakes, rivers, and pure white sand beaches. We stay at a hotel on Sunday. It is morning. I cannot sleep. Feeling the need to make a check on my spiritual to do list, I journey to the pool to read my Bible about the time church service starts in the 'hood. I sit down the only one in the quiet, serene, pool area. I seek the still small voice in the pages of God's word when the door squeaks. I hear the echoing slap, glop, slap, glop of dollar store slippers coming my way. I look down at my Bible, not reading, trying to prevent eye contact. Maybe it will go away and I can have some peace. Then plop! He sits in the vinyl chair across from me.

He wears a vintage yellowed undershirt and swim trunks. I sit staring at my Bible attempting to look spiritual and he says these words in an accusatory tone designed to engage an argument: "What are you, some kind of Christian?" Nuts. What do you say? "No, I am Secret Service on recon looking for Al Qaeda terrorist cells in the UP of Michigan. The Blueberry Festival of Paradise, Michigan posts a high alert code-red threat for a terrorist attack." Not having presence of mind I said, "Yes, I am a minister." That did it. Open the floodgates of heaven, tear down the levees in New Orleans because he began an assault on Christianity, the Bible, spirituality and the church for what seemed like hours. He took short, shallow breaths between sermon points and I tried to break away, but no. Gripped in a headlock of heated one-sided debate neither FEMA nor the National Guard could save me from this hurricane of hatred. I started to get angry. This is MY vacation. I felt rigid, whiny, difficult, and self-absorbed about being left alone.

Then a moment. He became exhausted from his tirade, like a hurricane diminishing to tropical storm status. I broke in and asked, "Excuse me sir, who hurt you?" He hung his head. He could not look up from the weight of his pain. He said in an articulate sullen tone, "A preacher . . . a preacher ran off with my wife, and I have never gotten over it." The wave recedes.

I grieved with him, encouraged and prayed for him. We discovered in the 'hood that behind angry, rigid, whiny, self-absorbed thinking is brokenness, deep woundedness of sin and shame. People cover their broken places with thought distortion, perfection, drugs, and alcohol to restore balance. If the brokenness can be discovered, named, then healing can happen. Not only healing, but the hurt becomes our strength. The very person or event in life which brought us to our knees now becomes the pathway for wholeness and strength. At this point of weakness pride recedes and God enters tenderly clothing shame with grace.

Paul the Apostle talks about this.

> *To keep me from becoming conceited because of these surpassingly great revelations, there was given me a thorn in my flesh, a messenger of Satan, to torment me. Three times I pleaded with the Lord to take it away from me. But he said to me, "My grace is sufficient for you, for my power is made perfect in weakness." Therefore I will boast all the more gladly about my weaknesses, so that Christ's power may rest on me. That is why, for Christ's sake, I delight in weaknesses, in insults, in hardships, in persecutions, in difficulties. For when I am weak, then I am strong. 2 Corinthians 12: 7-10 NIV*

Paul possessed incredible gifts from God. But deeper blessings than giftedness uncover in a growing spirituality-grace, power and inner strength in weakness. Paul's Tsunami impacted on a Damascus road on the way to persecute Christians. History, however, will remember him as Christ's greatest defender. God transformed his brokenness into tenderness for Christians. The broken place became God's strength.

Where have you been hurt? What is that place of anxiety for you? This becomes the fertile soil of God's power. Brokenness. Have religious folk fouled you when you tried to score? You drove the lane and a well-meaning leader clothes lined you. You were carried out of the narthex bleeding and broken. Opponents of Shaquille O'Neal have adopted a strategy against him. The Shaq doesn't shoot free throws well. Something about the physics of a 340-pound giant gently lofting pigskin at an iron rim doesn't compute. So, opponents commit Hack a Shaq. They foul him before he can slam-dunk. Let this be your place of power . . . caring and restoring victims of intentional flagrant fouls inflicted by perfect people. There will be no end to helping hurting hearts.

Our church community meets in brokenness. There are women who have lost children, through abortion and natural causes. They support each other from a broken heart. We have a healing ministry for addictions. The leadership comprises recovering people who found hope and help in Jesus Christ. Their greatest weakness has now become the power of their lives.

Anxiety reaction is at the core of addiction and sin. Worry wrapped its claws around the first family in the Garden of Eden. Man and woman react and attachments form, thinking distorts, death of relationship enters. God loves and seeks. He clothes with grace and kindness. God then empowers the first family in their weaknesses. He tells Eve that the treasure of her heart will be experienced in the strain of childbirth. The father exhorts Adam that the deeper meaning of work and creativity will be known in the ordeal of labor. He gives them gifts of honesty, truth, and richness of being in their frailty.

The power of Christian community emerges in her brokenness. Thought distortion disappears. You go deeper.

> *So, what do you think? With God on our side like this, how can we lose?*
> *If God didn't hesitate to put everything on the line for us, embracing our condition and exposing himself to the worst by sending His own Son, is there anything else he wouldn't gladly and freely do for us? And who would dare tangle with God by messing with one of God's chosen? Who would dare even to point a finger? The One who died for us—who was raised to life for us!—is in the presence of God at this very moment sticking up for us. Do you think anyone is going to be able to drive a wedge between us and Christ's love for us? There is no way! Not trouble, not hard times, not hatred, not hunger, not homelessness, not bullying threats, not backstabbing, not even the worst sins listed in Scripture:*
> *They kill us in cold blood because they hate you.*
> *We're sitting ducks; they pick us off one by one.*
> *None of this fazes us because Jesus loves us. I'm absolutely convinced that nothing—nothing living or dead, angelic or demonic, today or tomorrow, high or low, thinkable or unthinkable—absolutely nothing can get between us and God's love because of the way that Jesus our Master has embraced us.*
> *Romans 8:31-39 MSG*

Nothing can separate us from the love of God . . . he works it (our broken places) together for good. Pain possesses purpose. God does not squander suffering. Let your greatest weakness and sorrow become His power, the entry point for grace and wholeness. The Gospel story is experienced in brokenness.

Small Group Bible Study

Look at this Scripture. Talk with your group about your reflections on this passage. When we write your story tonight, we will discuss your own brokenness.

> *But this precious treasure-this light and power that now shine within us-is held in perishable containers, that is in our weak bodies. So everyone can see that our glorious power is from God and is not our own. We are pressed on every side by troubles, but we are not crushed and broken. We are perplexed but we don't give up and quit. We are hunted down but God never abandons us. We get knocked down but we get up again and keep going.*
> *2 Corinthians 4:7-9 NLT*

1. I think much of contemporary Christianity is too "me focused". In this passage you will find that our brokenness has another focal point. What is it . . . and how does it happen?

2. Great strength emerges in this passage. What is that strength?

3. Here is another strength in weakness passage. What is the purpose of our brokenness and weakness?

> *To keep me from becoming conceited because of these surpassingly great revelations, there was given me a thorn in my flesh, a messenger of Satan, to torment me. Three times I pleaded with the Lord to take it away from me. But he said to me, "My grace is sufficient for you, for my power is made perfect in weakness." Therefore I will boast all the more gladly about my weaknesses, so that Christ's power may rest on me. That is why, for Christ's sake, I delight in weaknesses, in insults, in hardships, in persecutions, in difficulties. For when I am weak, then I am strong.*
> *2 Corinthians 12: 7-10 NIV*

Writing Your Story, Healing Your Heart

This is one of the most important pieces of your story. Share with your group the broken places of your life which Jesus is transforming into His strengths. Be brutally truthful. Write the story of your brokenness and the hope that comes from your story of hurt. I trust that Clare's story will help you become more transparent than you may have been.

Clare's Story

While in college, I went to the doctor's office and consulted with my physician. I told her that I was always tired, spacey and unmotivated then I asked her if she could prescribe me some sort of energizing medicine. She asked me a few questions about my mental health and then handed me a diagnosis of depression and a six month supply of antidepressants.

Within three weeks I was regaining my energy and spunk. I began socializing with people who didn't remind me of my self-contrived and abundant flaws. I began to smoke a lot of marijuana, and drink a lot of alcohol. I made friends, and had the time of my life. During my senior year in college I started dating one of my room mates, Joshua. Within weeks of that relationship I found myself pregnant.

The edge of the bathtub felt cold through the seat of my jeans . . . the same sensation my face interpreted the night before against the seat of the toilet. Just the day before I had celebrated my twenty-first birthday and had a reasonable explanation for a late night with the porcelain god; my friends had taken me out on a '21 run' to several different bars and house parties, the extent of which I was unable to remember this morning. Tonight my state of mind was not quite so jovial as I looked into a reason behind my daily vomiting episodes this past month. My three house-mates continued to celebrate the weekend on the other side of this bathroom door as I handed over my future to my half ounce urine sample. A bright pink plus sign ignited fear in my spirit as it showed its incriminating face through the cheap view-window of the pregnancy test. The white plastic dipstick lay bearing its soul, my soul, on the lid of the toilet seat–and I put my face in my hands and cried.

I wrapped the test in an unreasonable amount of toilet paper and shoved it to the bottom of the waste basket. I opened the door and walked out into the living room flashing a forged smile at the company that had arrived while I was facing the facts in the bathroom. Nearly a dozen people, and an equal number of lit candles and incense, filled the tapestry clad room. I sat down on the couch with my knees folded to my chest and made a sad attempt at small talk.

"What's wrong, Clare?" one of my house-mates asked as one shoved a shot glass into my hands. They didn't care to know the answer to their generic question, and they didn't even care that I refused the sample of tequila.

I actually thought I had gotten away with passing on the booze until my other house-mate, Joshua, sat down beside me. He returned the shot class to my hands, "What do you think you're doing passing?"

Giving up drinking would be the easiest of my passions I'd have to forgo with this pregnancy. Last week I had just confirmed my long awaited trip to England taking a leave of absence from my first semester of my senior year, and paid my first months payment on the storage unit I'd rent for the twelve months I'd planned to be gone. I pondered traveling to England with a pregnancy unbeknownst to everyone.

"I just don't feel well yet." I said unleashing the emotion behind my sick stomach.

"Well, drink this," he said "it will make you feel better!" His comment emphasized the fact that he wasn't ready to take responsibility for his adult life–nonetheless this baby's. How was I going to tell him I was pregnant with his child? How was our relationship–barely peaking four months–going to bare this burden?

Burden? I thought, what kind of understatement is that? "I'm going to go l lie down." I uttered as I made my way to the room we shared. I curled up in the fetal position on our queen-sized bed–the same bed Joshua and I had probably conceived this baby in. I felt sick, I felt sad, I felt scared. I wanted my own room–I wanted yesterday back.

A walk-in appointment at my university clinic confirmed the truth behind my worst fear. I cried into the mannequin arms of the nurse as she explained "the options" to me in a dull, monotone, voice. The options, I thought to myself as I drove back and forth along the campus. The finals I was skipping were the least of my worries as I contemplated abortion, adoption, and parenthood.

Sunset led my Jetta back to another night in the house I shared with my friend on Maple Street. I again found myself turning down Tequila shots as I joined those steadfast guests in my house–but wasn't as effective in my attempt at emotional stability. Immediately upon entering the bedroom I burst into body-shaking tears and re-familiarized the side of my face with the white cotton pillowcase covering my very own pillow.

"Sweetie, what is wrong with you?" It was Joshua's voice. He had followed me into the bedroom and was now lying beside me on the green and red striped comforter his grandmother had made him when he was in high school.

"Nothing" I managed to lie between sniffles.

"Oh my God, are you pregnant?" he asked completely out of the blue.

"What?!" I gasped, appalled at hearing those words out loud, "No! Why? What if I were?!" I slipped.

He knew I was trying to delay the inevitable. He put his hands to his face and ran out of the room. I could hear him down the hall in the bathroom . . . puking with the truth in his assumption. I wasn't sure whether I felt relief that I had told him, or regret that I could not turn back. We spent that night tossing and turning and avoiding body contact at all costs—as if it would compensate for previous flesh matrimony.

I was within a year of receiving a bachelor's degree in psychology and enrolling in midwifery school. I was twenty-one years old; old enough to take responsibility for my actions. I knew that if I gave this baby up I would be reminded of it everyday of my life—an issue I wasn't sure my history of clinical depression could handle.

I'd been on anti-depressants for several years, and staying pregnant would mean I'd have to go off of them. This is a step I'd considered before, but my fear of relapse compelled me to continue taking that darn yellow pill every morning.

The next week brought concerned advice from my room mates and their parents to give the baby up for adoption—while my family and my heart occupied my other shoulder with convincing counsel to carry and raise this child.

I spent the summer single, and in summer school. Joshua and I broke up after he expressed his fear over fatherhood, and I insisted on doing it alone. I stopped popping my antidepressants, and I felt good in that aspect. However, I cried with my hormone overload the day my passport came in the mail, and I wore baggy clothes to hide the expansion in my waist—embarrassed that those nameless frat-party-regulars I used to get drunk with might recognize me and jump to lewd conclusions.

By the time fall semester of my senior year rolled around I was obviously pregnant and was forced to trade my catwalk for a confident waddle. Overloading with six classes gave me so much to think about that I didn't have time to care about the whispers I imagined behind my back, and the life I'd lead as a single parent in December.

I'd sit through classes with my unfamiliar body crammed sideways into the desk seats made for the skinny body my soul previously resided in. The professors would profess 'that which made the world go 'round' and I'd sit as their student, feel the baby kick within my body, and dispute their wisdom—wondering if they had any children themselves.

Joshua and I would occasionally hang out together and he'd come to all the ultra sound appointments at the doctors office. Each image he saw of the baby would soften his fears a little more—and I could see in his eyes that he wanted this baby to be a part of his life.

"This baby is made up of you and me," he said as the prenatal heart beat echoed through the monitor in the obstetrics clinic. The monitor revealed the tiny hands and feet of the life I was carrying. This was my future now—this monitor shed light on my life like no GPA ever could. I traded backpacks for diaper-bags and theme parties for baby showers.

Finals week was approaching as quickly as my due date—and I was racing to settle my nest before the baby's birth. As November handed off to December—Joshua professed his undying love and devotion to me, and managed to support these claims with regular backrubs.

"I think I'm having contractions." I said the Sunday night before my first final. "Okay, uhm, we've gotta' time them," he said, trying to remember all the things the doctor told us to do when we thought 'it was time.' Twenty minutes apart. This was nothing to get excited about—we were looking for 5 minute intervals.

I woke up beside Joshua at 4:00 a.m. and I said, "I can't sleep." "Me neither." He put his arm around the part of my body that used to be my waist. It was just the three of us there—sorta.'

Monday morning. I made it through my first final devoting the entire two hour period to not focusing on the imminent birth of this baby. Tuesday was a repeat of Monday—the only difference being that now I had two finals finished.

7:00 a.m. Wednesday, December 17th. I was admitted into the hospital for induction of labor. By 7:30 a.m. the waiting room was filled with the support of my family and our tequila-drinking-friends. In between mind altering contractions Joshua and I discussed marriage, and McDonald's Breakfast sandwiches. I was clenching his arm and doing all I could to manage a drug-free labor. The only pain-relief I wanted in my room was the soothing sound of the 'music of Ireland' CD playing beside my delivery bed. I remember 10:13 a.m.

> when she placed your new wet body on my
> sweat-sparkled chest - heaving with your seven pound six ounce entirety.
> I remember the image
> with my desires
> with my fears
> with my fistful of ultra-sound photos
> simply disappeared into a much greater reality.
> I remember
> with an overwhelming relief previously unknown,
> eye contact with perfection -
> and a choir of angels played in my background as I spoke
> over and over
> the only words that would come to my lips
> "you are so beautiful, baby"
> "you are so beautiful."

"Josh, will you go ask my professors if I can take my last two finals here in the hospital?" I asked, clutching our new son, River, against my chest. Josh looked into my determined eyes, and put his finger into River's tiny hand.

"I'm so proud of you," he said, letting the delivery-inspired tears roll down his cheek and off of his chin into our lives. "Yeah, I'll do that for you," he looked at the new life we held in our eyes, "look what you did for me."

I took my remaining two finals in the hospital on Thursday and Friday—it was the end of my last semester as an independent woman. I was beginning a new life just like this baby I held in my arms—and it would revolve around him, and his life would revolve around mine. We would go 'round and 'round together and I felt intoxicated from his love.

River My Life
I hold life giving water in meditation
while I contemplate the meaning of my world.
His new cerulean eyes make known wisdom in a depth,
a concentrated intense body in which I will baptize myself with his
saturating charisma.
River currents ebb in the cleft of his chin
and my heart melts into that cloven space
when I lay my nose against the vast splendor of his cheeks
and inhale, smell, breathe, the sweetness of his salt-speckled child-flesh.
I beg for your secrets, and you scream for me,
your gaze is my fellowship, and I hold you, rock you, in my arms.
The moon sets over your eyelids and the blood-water of your veins flow
from life giving water of your person to the river of my soul,
and in my meditation your face reveals to me my purpose.

Josh and I were married, and divorced a year later. After months of empty promises and lies that he had quit all drugs completely, and wasn't selling them, I got a telephone call from one of his friends. "Clare," the friend said "I have decided to call you and tell you something because I like you a lot and I know you have a new baby in the house and I don't think it is right that Josh is lying to you." My heart was pounding. "Go out and look in the large blue bin in the garage." So I did. In the blue bin I found several pounds of marijuana measured out into baggies, along side several smoking pipes and elaborate glass bongs. I grabbed them and ran into the bathroom and began dumping them all into the toilet and flushing. Joshua discovered me irate in the bathroom.

"You liar! I hate you! I hate you! This marriage is over! You Liar!" and with each flush I told myself how stupid I was for believing him when he told me that he wasn't selling pot, wasn't smoking pot, and didn't have any pot.

Josh began pulling handfuls of wet marijuana out of the toilet "stop flushing! Please, you are wasting it! You know how much money this is??"

Then I ran to the garage and began throwing the glass paraphernalia onto the cement floor, assuring that they each broke into hundreds of little pieces; like my heart. Then I handed him the broom, grabbed River out of his crib, and drove three hours to my mom's house. I rented an apartment in her complex and we raised our babies together. I began working as a bartender, with my expensive college degree in my back pocket. But at least I was standing up for what I believed in.

When River turned five years old, I got pregnant again by Max the bartender whom I worked with. In November 2002 I had another son, Alex. Max and I also married, and divorced within a year for nearly the same reasons. Max was addicted to drugs, and pornography, and lying about both. I caught him hiding his pornography in our son's nursery closet. Of course he swore it wasn't his.

I secretly tested his urine for drugs with an at-home urine drug test. He swore the positive result had to have been in error. He promised me the pot that I repeatedly found under the seat of his car, and in the pockets of his coat was his friends.

I became a labor and delivery nurse, and kicked Max out of my house. He moved in with a friend and continued his addictions. River, age 5 at the time, told me that he didn't like Max. I took full custody of our son, and sold the house. I moved in with a guy friend of mine who later became a boyfriend. When I discovered him cheating on me shortly thereafeter, I rented my own place on the lake and committed to a year of being single with my kids and healing some wounds.

I began seeing a counselor, travelling the world, painting, and exercising. I felt healthy in every way. My kids were thriving and beautiful. Above all else I wanted to show them that I would never put a man before them, and that it was not okay for them to put up with abuse from a partner. I wanted my kids to feel loved and safe and valuable. I wanted my kids to know that their hearts mattered to me.

Write Your Story Of Brokenness

Write Your Story

Prayer Heals the Heart

God grant me the serenity
to accept the things I cannot change;
courage to change the things I can;
and wisdom to know the difference.
-Reinhold Niebuhr

MILLIONS OF PEOPLE talk to God using the Serenity Prayer every day. This passionate plea unearths pure gold; serenity, courage, and the shoe leather of transformation-wisdom. Prayer holds a high place in the healing heart. At some painful point brokenness pours out fervent words to something or someone for help. The amazing consequence for millions today . . . God answers anxious angst. He exists and cares about tangled messes. The psalmist says it well. When we pray, "God sends His word and he heals. He gets us out in the "nick of time." Check out this beautiful song in Psalm 107.10-22:

Some of you were locked in a dark cell,
cruelly confined behind bars,
Punished for defying God's Word,
for turning your back on the High God's counsel–
A hard sentence, and your hearts so heavy,
and not a soul in sight to help.
Then you called out to God in your desperate condition;
He got you out in the nick of time.
He led you out of your dark, dark cell,

broke open the jail and led you out.
So thank God for His marvelous love,
for His miracle mercy to the children He loves;
He shattered the heavy jailhouse doors,
He snapped the prison bars like matchsticks!

Some of you were sick because you'd lived a bad life,
your bodies feeling the effects of your sin;
You couldn't stand the sight of food,
so miserable you thought you'd be better off dead.
Then you called out to God in your desperate condition;
He got you out in the nick of time.
He spoke the word that healed you,
that pulled you back from the brink of death.
So thank God for his marvelous love,
for His miracle mercy to the children He loves.
MSG

When we form the word in our mouth, "God" intimate connection happens. Perceived distance becomes experienced nearness. The divine touches human. The healer of the heart connects with marvelous love and miracle mercy to the children he adores.

I often sit with my laptop in coffee shops. A small window in the lower right corner of the liquid crystal diode screen tells me an internet network engages. Defeat grips when the Arial font window informs that no link exists. "No connection for you, dude." I cannot tell you the delight when the window says, "Network connection in range. You are now connected." Friend, when you pray, God links up and communication happens!

Prayer begins the healing journey. You can pray any time anxiety escalates. When you want to use, when you feel like hiding, believe you are a nothing, a failure . . . pray and God listens. Do you remember listening as a treasure? He pays attention. In prayer, reach out to the heart of God and he passionately touches in return.

A tough biker called and asked to meet. I felt a bit nervous. He stood over six feet tall, pony tail, with a *la familia mafiosa* look. He took off his trench coat, sat down in my living room, and poured out his heart. The gangster listed six things in his life melting down like a nuclear reactor. He also declared that he did not believe in God. I don't do this often, but I challenged him and said, "Let's pray for all six items and see what God does. If the Lord does nothing, then don't believe in Him." Perhaps the statement was arrogant, but I felt that prayer framed the only hope for this man at the time. Within a month God answered all six prayers, managed the meltdowns, and the large *godfatheresque* biker came to faith. Not long ago he called to report cancer filled his body. He felt happy that God injected him with hope at each intravenous chemo therapy session. Me too.

Please don't be fooled by political propaganda and media circus misdirection. People pray . . . a lot. According to Gallup 90 percent of Americans pray. 75 percent pray daily because prayer possesses power. Over 80 percent of Americans favor an amendment to restore prayer to public schools (New York Times).

Something happened in America since the 1962 Supreme Court declared prayer unconstitutional in schools thereby removing prayer from the classroom. A mentor of mine remembers when public schools gladly welcomed prayer to begin each day. The greatest behavior problems he saw in students at that time were tardiness, gum chewing, and spit wads. Some genius pushed the infamous idea through the highest court in the land to excise prayer from public schools. Since the prayerectomy, chewing gum and spitting paper would be welcomed distractions compared to bullets, barbiturates, and bomb laden backpacks. Not such a supreme decision in my court of opinion. A friend sent this to me recently.

After being interviewed by the school administration, a   new teaching prospect   said, "Let me see if I've got this right: You want me to go into that room with all those kids, correct their disruptive behavior, observe them for signs of abuse, monitor their dress habits, censor their T-shirt messages, and instill in them a love for learning.   You want me to check their backpacks for weapons, wage war on drugs and sexually transmitted diseases, and raise their sense of self esteem and personal pride.

You want me to teach them patriotism and good citizenship, sportsmanship and fair play, and how to register to vote, balance a checkbook, and apply for a job.   You want me to check their heads for lice, recognize signs of antisocial behavior, and make sure that they all pass the state exams. You want me to provide them with an equal education regardless of their handicaps, and communicate regularly with their parents by letter, telephone, newsletter, and report card. You want me to do all this with a piece of chalk, a blackboard, a bulletin board, a few books, a big smile, and a starting salary that qualifies me for food stamps. You want me to do all this and then you tell me . . . . I CAN'T PRAY?"

Sonorous prayer resounds through broken hearts. Hurt people sense loss of control when someone rips choices away. Prayer begins to fill the void of powerlessness. Wounded hearts speak to God and emptiness disappears. So, prayer forms on lips again.

The majority of hurt people with whom I have worked tell stories of family failure. A parent disappointed and hurt them. A mother who twists healthy sexuality teaching children the value of pornography, control, or rage can facilitate lost and disconnected feelings. Attachments form and he seeks someone or something to fill the void and dull the pain. The child reacts to family anxiety and develops ways of coping which damage other relationships and the injury goes deeper. The result is one more generation of wounded children. The treasure of prayer begins to rewire broken hearts from wounded families by connecting us to God, our Father.

Let me show you how this rewiring takes place in the Lord's Prayer and what I call Jesus' "Great Prayer" of John 17. In these two prayers Jesus touches the deepest of all anxieties, father hunger.

Matthew 6.9-13
Our Father in heaven,
Hallowed be Your name.
Your kingdom come.
Your will be done
On earth as it is in heaven.
Give us this day our daily bread.
And forgive us our debts,
As we forgive our debtors.
And do not lead us into temptation,
But deliver us from the evil one.
For Yours is the kingdom and the power and the glory forever. Amen.
NKJV

Through prayer Jesus leads us into the presence of the perfect parent. God is "The Father". Jesus loved the term using it over 200 times in the Gospels because this name embodies the end of our search for meaning and fulfillment. Victor Frankl survived the horror of Nazi concentration camps. As he reflected on his torture within a death culture, he came to the conclusion that finding God forms the deepest significance of life. In this prayer the Son gently guides us to this meaning by teaching us to pray . . . Father.

Addiction and trauma metaphorically cross wires in our brain. The hard wiring sends us to seek solace in substances and ill relationships. The victim of sexual assault often pursues promiscuity or an opposite aversion to sex. The answer is not steps at this point, or a seminar on esteem building. Intimate relationship with God rewires the broken paradigm. The fatherhood of God cherishes hurt people without condition. The perfect parent protects, and draws near to embrace through prayer.

In the Sermon on the Mount two caveats precede Christ's teaching on rewiring prayer. First, He wishes that we not pray for performance points. Secondly, He challenges us to pray deeper than religious folk who ask God for quantity and not quality. Look at His words in Matthew 6.5.

"When you pray, don't be like the hypocrites who love to pray publicly on street corners and in the synagogues where everyone can see them. I tell you the truth; that is all the reward they will ever get. But when you pray, go away

by yourself, shut the door behind you, and pray to your Father in private.
Then your Father, who sees everything, will reward you.
"When you pray, don't babble on and on as people of other religions do. They
think their prayers are answered merely by repeating their words again and
again. Don't be like them, for your Father knows exactly what you need even
before you ask Him! Pray like this:
(NLT)

When I pray, sometimes I wonder if my entreaties attempt to manipulate God and direct the affection of people to approve my spirituality. Jesus instead teaches us how to pray for the fatherhood of God.

Next, Jesus emphasizes how to pray. He connects purpose to prayer. He says this in Matthew 6.9 as he mentors His leadership team, "In this manner, therefore, pray." The Greek New Testament uses emphatic words in this purpose statement painting a type of ancient exclamation point. Jesus says, "Pray this way friends!"

Regularly I try to listen to the words that come out of my mouth when I pray. At times I hear, "blah, blah, blah." I wonder if this is a futile attempt to get my prayer time in so God likes me more. This all feels quite empty. When I don't know how to pray, I ask for the Father. I bury my face deep into His chest and seek divine embrace. His nearness helps me recover from the performance plan pounding out tiring transactions to win approval.

When we pray, Father, he begins to touch the deepest of all anxieties, the hunger for father. Look at the prologue of the Lord's Prayer and The Great Prayer.

Our Father in heaven
Matthew 6.9-13

After saying all these things, Jesus looked up to heaven and said, "Father, ... ".
John 17.1

The four horsemen of anxiety are existential, neurotic, historic, and father hunger. The Lord's Prayer and the Great Prayer bring peace to the deepest of anxieties, the driving need for a father's love. Dr. Margo Maine in her book, *Father Hunger,* identifies the broken relationship of a biological father with a daughter as the catalyst for eating disorders. She states that 8 percent of women suffer from addictive attachments to food. (Maine, p. xiii) Maine traces the root cause of anorexia and bulimia to relationship disappointment between father and child. Dr. Maine deserves great applause for her work. I believe however that her book does not go deep enough. No father can be a perfect parent for a daughter. Father hunger plunges deeper than paternity. This chronic anxiety touches the need of every person to be cherished by God the Father. When we choose not to finish the equation of intimacy with God, unquenching hunger can devastate our nervous system. Anxiety escalates. A woman then controls the one thing in life she can have power over, food intake.

Sam Osherson too identifies father hunger as a core anxiety. He states that the greatest underestimated tragedy of our time is the emotional or physical absence of the father. In a survey of over 7,000 men almost none of them were close to their fathers. The distance between father and son creates frustration and inner upheaval. In a study on men in positions of power they have done well in jobs almost intuitively but have showed confusion about intimate issues of their lives like wives, kids, and parents. The arena of love confused them most. Men carry a void of vulnerability, dependency and emptiness because of broken relationship with their biological father. Jesus begins to connect the dots between our innate need to love God and to be cherished by Him through prayer. There are a number of symptoms of father hunger; phoniness, pleasing through working more, dusty rigid rules, and anger. (Osherson, pp. 5-6) Could it be that the Lord's Prayer specifically, and prayer in general bring us to an intimacy with God as Father? Is it possible that the deepest longing of mankind is to connect with the fatherhood of God?

Let me show you a few ways Jesus connects us to God as Father through prayer. In the Lord's Prayer Jesus opens the door to proximity and presence with the intimate word a child speaks to a parent. Father is pronounced abba in Jesus' dialect, the sound an infant makes when calling its parent.

In the Great Prayer of John 17, approximately 100 pronouns of I, me, yours, and mine show proximity of Jesus to the Father. In the Greek New Testament many of these pronouns like "you" and "me" place next to each other. When you read the Greek, you see the proximity and intimacy of Jesus to the Father. Jesus calms our greatest anxiety with the presence of the perfect parent, God.

*John 17.4**εγωσε**εδοξασαεπιτηςγηςτοεργοντελειωσαςοδεδωκαςμοιιναποιησω*
*5και νυν δοξασον **με συ** πατερ παρα σεαυτω τη δοξη η ειχον προ του τον κοσμον ειναι παρα σοι*

Note how the pronouns in bold, I and you, pronounced *ego* and *se* in verse 4 and *me* and *su* of verse 5 stand next to each other. I glorified you. You glorify me. I echoed you, you mirror me. I honored you, now you reflect me. Prayer begins to untangle the mess of our lives with intimate connection to the presence of God the Father.

The common theme woven through both the Lord's Prayer and the Great Prayer is the power of intimacy with God, that special place where humans and God meet satisfying the hunger for Father. In the Great Prayer of John 17 Jesus affirms the relationship. *You are father . . . we are one.* The connection with the Father completes. He does not ask for long lists of things for Himself. The proximity of their relationship forms His focus in prayer. He prays as though nearness to God becomes all we need. Calling out to God, as Father, opens the door to intimate community.

A powerful truth of father hunger emerges here, a treasure. The Scriptures never mention Jesus' stepfather, Joseph, after the birth accounts of Matthew and Luke. Joseph was not present at Jesus' inauguration of ministry or His crucifixion. History has no record of Joseph so either he left his family or died. Joseph, Jesus' stepfather, left whether by choice or by death. Jesus lived with a void of an earthly father's presence. Though fully God, Christ was completely man and susceptible to the anxieties attached to the need for a father. I wonder if this answers the "why" these words run so consistent in His prayers. Jesus connected with the fatherhood of God in the absence of an earthly father.

In my daughter's junior year of high school she came home one evening and made a beeline for my neck. Her body language and different gate triggered instant concern. Wrapping her arms around me she sobbed deeply into my chest. "Daddy, he broke up with me." As I write this, tears swell. I have never seen her so devastated and alone. The despair in her pleas for comfort and help still haunt me. I held her until the heaving stopped and my shirt saturated with tears.

Human beings cannot meet the deepest longings for love and acceptance. Only in the arms of the heavenly Father can profound wounds be touched. Only God can. There is great freedom here. Did your parents hurt you? Did she abuse you? When parents disappoint and lovers leave, one intimate relationship holds the power to fill and heal. God, the Father.

Another aspect of prayer comes out in the word, Father . . . power when the world goes crazy.

The word for pray comes from the latin word, precarious. This part of the prayer is what I call "911 prayer" . . . when the world falls precariously on top of you.

I love true dispatcher stories. Check these out.

Dispatcher: 9-1-1 What is the nature of your emergency?
Caller: I'm trying to reach nine eleven but my phone doesn't have an eleven on it.
Dispatcher: This is nine eleven.
Caller: I thought you just said it was nine-one-one.
Dispatcher: Yes, ma'am nine-one-one and nine-eleven are the same thing.
Caller: Honey, I may be old, but I'm not stupid.
Dispatcher: 9-1-1 What's the nature of your emergency?
Caller: My wife is pregnant and her contractions are only two minutes apart.
Dispatcher: Is this her first child?
Caller: No, you idiot! This is her husband!
And the winner is . . . .
Dispatcher: 9-1-1
Caller: Yeah, I'm having trouble breathing. I'm all out of breath. Darn . . . . I think I'm going to pass out.

Dispatcher: Sir, where are you calling from?
Caller: I'm at a pay phone. North and Foster.
Dispatcher: Sir, an ambulance is on the way. Are you an asthmatic?
Caller: No.
Dispatcher: What were you doing before you started having trouble breathing?
Caller: Running from the Police.

When your parent disappoints and you feel the anxiety of disappointment and grief, this Father cannot fail. I see Christians and friends in recovery carrying loads of grief over their parents. They remain unhealed and feel disconnected because of the sins of their earthly father. So Jesus gives us the Father in prayer. There is nothing greater than His presence. Jesus brings you to him. Anxiety diminishes. He has the power to carry you through the 911 storms of life, he asks you to let Him. You can know this in prayer.

Ever need prayer dispatch? I love how King David thought about God when he prayed. Look at his reflection of the Father in Psalm 62.

> *Let all that I am wait quietly before God,*
> *for my hope is in Him.*
> *He **alone** is my rock and my salvation,*
> *my fortress where I will not be shaken.*
> *My victory and honor come from God **alone.***
> *He is my refuge, a rock where no enemy can reach me.*
> *O my people, trust in Him at all times.*
> *Pour out your heart to Him,*
> *for God is our refuge.*
> *Psalm 62.5*

6 times the word "alone", or "only" in some translations, appear in this Psalm. David masterfully focuses his prayer on the "only" one who can touch the deepest needs of his life. David also uses prepositions to drive home the "only" nature of God the Father. When you examine the Hebrew text, it literally says in verses 5-7, "My hope is **from within** Him. My honor is **upon** Him, the rock of my strength is **in Him**." The vision is the Father . . . from this vantage point you can see clearly through the crisis of dispatch days and 911 nights. You can experience His love from within, upon, and in the Father alone. David's prayer emerges from his need of the Father's power.

King David had many talents but he was especially skilled at being left alone through abandonment and betrayal. Scripture breathes little about David's biological father, Jesse. David as leader apparently did not know Jesse's ongoing mentorship. David's father in law, Saul, tried to pin him to the wall with a spear hoping David would terminally get the King's point. David's wife, Michal, like

Simon the American Idol judge, criticized her husband declaring he would never make it in showbiz. Afterward the only thing Michal and David consummated was a painful political pact. Absalom, David's son, which means "my father of peace", attempted to over throw his dad in a military coup. Absalom tried to wash the king's superstardom out of his long hair, but got hung out to dry. David had a tough life . . . you wouldn't want it. But you would desire David's vision of God when his crazy family conspired, abandoned, and betrayed him. *"Let all I am wait quietly . . . my hope is in Him."* Focus shifts from insanity to the perspective of the Father who rewires family tragedy. Perhaps the brokenness of David's family life opened doors to deeper dispatch prayers.

One last 911 prayer . . . literally. Look at Psalm **91.1** through 91.16.

Psalm 91.1 (911)

Those who live in the shelter of the Most High
will find rest in the shadow of the Almighty.
This I declare about the LORD:
He alone is my refuge, my place of safety;
He is my God, and I trust Him.
For He will rescue you from every trap
and protect you from deadly disease.
He will cover you with His feathers.
He will shelter you with His wings.
His faithful promises are your armor and protection.
Do not be afraid of the terrors of the night,
nor the arrow that flies in the day.
Do not dread the disease that stalks in darkness,
nor the disaster that strikes at midday.
Though a thousand fall at your side,
though ten thousand are dying around you,
these evils will not touch you.
Just open your eyes,
and see how the wicked are punished.
If you make the LORD your refuge,
if you make the Most High your shelter,
no evil will conquer you;
no plague will come near your home.
For He will order His angels
to protect you wherever you go.
They will hold you up with their hands
so you won't even hurt your foot on a stone.
You will trample upon lions and cobras;
you will crush fierce lions and serpents under your feet!

The LORD says, "I will rescue those who love me.
I will protect those who trust in my name.
When they call on me, I will answer;
I will be with them in trouble.
I will rescue and honor them.
I will reward them with a long life
and give them my salvation."

Fishing fills my free time and thoughts. I love fly and spin casting . . . you name it. I have a handcrafted golden hued wooden drift boat with green trim. Lori and I enjoy romantic rides and fishing adventures. I fish . . . she looks beautiful. We return renewed. I trolled on a nearby lake for trout. Though a slow day for catching, I finally landed a rainbow with the hook set deep in the gills. I tried to save the silver and pink striped beauty, but no luck. Although I have been seen kissing fish on the lips, mouth to mouth on trout doesn't work well. I slipped the deceased into the water watching the carcass bob up and down as I motored away. My boat moved 5 meters away from the burial at sea when I heard what sounded like a freight train behind my left shoulder. Startled, I jerked back and saw the most lovely sight I have ever seen. A bald eagle with a 6 foot wing span had been watching my fruitless fishing. When I landed the catch and then returned it to the lake, the dark brown eagle swooped. The great bird soared so close I saw the subtle separations between the long thin feathers. As he struck the prey, his white head and broad tail seemed brilliantly iridescent. The dive velocity plunged the clawed feet of the immense eagle deep into the clear blue water. His gaze fierce and focused he ascended up and to my right on powerful wings. I sat stoically amazed unable to move. The grand bird flew over the horizon tightly clutching its catch in razor talons. Adrenalin reaction replaced boredom and I no longer felt alone. While I trolled without success, feeling sorry for myself, a powerful presence watched with great intensity. When I think the worst, when dreams collapse, when I choose not to engage God, the Father watches and waits. Vision is everything. Prayer opens my eyes to His greatness and presence.

The Father connection and rewiring from our hurt began at the cross. Roman soldiers pierced God capillaries and messiah veins ruptured. The heart of the Father pumped divine DNA covering the disgrace of shame. The result . . . honor. For every hurt person suffering the detonation of broken fatherhood look at Jesus' focus as he faces the cross.

After saying all these things, Jesus looked up to heaven and said, "Father, the hour has come. Glorify (honor) your Son so He can give glory (honor) back to you. For, you have given Him authority over everyone. He gives eternal life to each one you have given Him. And this is the way to have eternal life–to know you, the only true God, and Jesus Christ, the one you sent to earth. I

brought glory (honor) to you here on earth by completing the work you gave
me to do. Now, Father, bring me into the glory (honor) we shared before the
world began.
John 17.1-5

The word glory holds dual meaning . . . honor and powerful presence. The Old Testament *kabod* means heavy with honor. The New Testament *doxa* reflects God's presence to the point that one breaks out into praise and adoration . . . honor. Listen to the psalmist reflect on the presence and honor of God.

"Be still, and know that I am God! I will be honored by every nation.
I will be honored throughout the world."
Psalm 46:10

The fatherhood of God renews dishonor with honor when one prays. Christmas day 2005 Army Specialist Tony Cardinal patrolled the streets of Baghdad. He maneuvered the tan camo painted humvee through barricaded streets littered with debris from one of the most violent cultures in history. Ten days before his return to the states from Iraq his thoughts drifted from mid eastern chaos to kissing the infant daughter he had never seen. On route the detonation of an improvised explosive device shattered his dreams.

I received the call to perform Tony's memorial service, but did not immediately understand the enormity of the event. A one star general leading a corps of the Army's finest met with city officials and me to coordinate the plans. Tony's body would be honored in a memorial service at our church building and then transported by way of a horse drawn carriage to the cemetery. On the day of the funeral two long fire trucks with ladders unfurled a 30 foot flag over the entrance to the church parking lot. News media crews milled like paparazzi. The one star general and team of soldiers made every detail holy. During the ceremony the decorated general bent a knee and presented the young widow with Tony's medals. He softly spoke private words of strength to her as she wept into the neck of her swaddled infant daughter.

The ceremony was gripping, but the end got me. After a packed auditorium paid tribute, over 50 veterans of foreign wars marched by the casket to give the young hero honor. An aged WW2 vet carrying an oxygen tank in his left arm like a football gimped on clicking cartilage toward the casket. With his brown VFW cap tilted to one side the crooked veteran proudly displayed his medals on a vest far too small for his vast frame. He shuffled to the coffin, adjusted his O2 canister, stood over the young man . . . and saluted. In that instant, the aged veteran reflected the passion of a hero, his bent body looked different, reverent in the presence of one who shed his blood for others. In that crystalline moment, the veteran honored the hero and the thousands of men and women who gave their lives so we might be free. I felt fragile and small, as though 200 years of freedom hung in the balance of one man's gesture.

The carriage procession to the frozen cemetery took nearly an hour, the horses' hooves clopping hollow monotonous cadence. Tony's wife did not allow media at the open grave; only heaven records such events. At the graveside, every word, each intimation moved slow, solemn and sacred. The soldiers stood at attention in sub freezing temperature. I sat with family members silently waiting vigil as pride and passion lowered Tony's body into the earth. I will never be the same because of the powerful presence of honor.

A young father shed his blood for freedom. Jesus too reflects the honor of the Father when his blood shed for you. The glory and honor of Jesus replaces dishonor with honor.

Shame detonates and searing shrapnel pierces fragile hearts. Prayer begins to renew what terrorists rip away . . . honor. I see something in marriages that pray . . . in single people who pray . . . in the purity of people who pray . . . the presence of honor. Look at the Great Prayer of John 17 with me.

"My prayer is not for the world, but for those you have given me, because they belong to you. All who are mine belong to you, and you have given them to me, so they bring me glory (honor).
"I have given them the glory (honor) you gave me, so they may be one as we are one. I am in them and you are in me. May they experience such perfect unity that the world will know that you sent me and that you love them as much as you love me. Father, I want these whom you have given me to be with me where I am. Then they can see all the glory (honor) you gave me because you loved me even before the world began!

Listen to His words. Imagine the lazy Galilean dialect. "They were always yours. They belong to you. May they be one . . . may they have unity." Jesus possessed a serious sense of connection with God the Father as he faced the trauma of the cross. Examine the prayers of one who lays down His life. He focuses on the fatherhood of God. Nearness renews honor for dishonor. Hunger for the Father shrinks in powerful reverent connection.

Praying the fatherhood of God causes other scriptures to make more sense to me.

Pray in the Spirit at all times and on every occasion. Stay alert and be persistent in your prayers for all believers everywhere.
Ephesians 6:18

Never stop praying. 1 Thessalonians 5:17

These passages pray for His fatherhood on every occasion. Intimacy with the perfect Father rewires my crazy family pain, and renews dishonor replacing hurt with honor.

Hallowed Be Your Name . . . Father

Now Jesus pours on power. In the Lord's prayer He teaches us to pray the most potent piece of God's fatherhood . . . holy. Jesus not only prays "holy" in the Lord's Prayer, but He also declares this in the Great Prayer of John 17.

John 17.11-12
Holy Father, you have given me your name; now protect them by the power of your name so that they will be united just as we are. During my time here, I protected them by the power of the name you gave me. I guarded them so that not one was lost, except the one headed for destruction, as the Scriptures foretold.

In the Great Prayer Jesus calls the Father, Holy. He connects the intimacy of Father and Holy to power and unity. Let's look at where the Holy Name comes from in the book of Isaiah.

Isaiah 6
It was in the year King Uzziah died that I saw the Lord. He was sitting on a lofty throne, and the train of His robe filled the Temple. Attending Him were mighty seraphim, each having six wings. With two wings they covered their faces, with two they covered their feet, and with two they flew. They were calling out to each other,
"Holy, holy, holy is the Lord of Heaven's Armies!
The whole earth is filled with His glory!"
Their voices shook the Temple to its foundations, and the entire building was filled with smoke.
Then I said, "It's all over! I am doomed, for I am a sinful man. I have filthy lips, and I live among a people with filthy lips. Yet I have seen the King, the Lord of Heaven's Armies."
Then one of the seraphim flew to me with a burning coal he had taken from the altar with a pair of tongs. He touched my lips with it and said, "See, this coal has touched your lips. Now your guilt is removed, and your sins are forgiven."
Then I heard the Lord asking, "Whom should I send as a messenger to this people? Who will go for us?"
I said, "Here I am. Send me."

Look at Isaiah's experience. He has a vision, in his dream Isaiah dialogues with God's messengers . . . they speak to him and Isaiah's sin exposes and God transforms his failure with forgiveness. Some scholars will argue that biblical messengers represent the person of God Himself. The Father draws near, He touches and makes clean.

He touched my lips with it and said, "See, this coal has touched your lips.
Now your guilt is removed, and your sins are forgiven."

When we pray the Holy, defenses lower. The true self emerges so God can touch. This can only happen in prayer. Pride strips away and I see myself for what I am.

Pride begins with shame. Feeling disconnection with God and others shame hides to protect self and cover failure. Some hurt people literally disappear and shut people out. Others control image to hide. On the far end of the continuum shame steps up on a pedestal declaring to the world, "I am bigger and better, you can't hurt me." This same emotion drives the need to cover, simply in a different direction. This type of shame is pride. Try to knock the addict or victim off the pedestal, and pride entrenches protecting itself further. Prayer connects with God's Holy fatherhood. The holy takes our hand helping us down from the pedestal of pride. Look at the transparency and power of prayer in Psalm 139.

For the choir director: A psalm of David.
O Lord, you have examined my heart
and know everything about me.
You know when I sit down or stand up.
You know my thoughts even when I'm far away.
You see me when I travel
and when I rest at home.
You know everything I do.
You know what I am going to say
even before I say it, Lord.
You go before me and follow me.
You place your hand of blessing on my head.
Such knowledge is too wonderful for me,
too great for me to understand!

A biker came to Christ, his name, Jim Nyberg. His conversion was dramatic. He joined my small group. Two months after he came to Christ Jim's doctor informed him of a prognosis, lung cancer. He began chemo and radiation, 5 days a week. The therapy burnt his esophagus. He could no longer eat nor drink. Our group prayed for him often, and I wondered if his faith would falter because he was a new believer.

One day Jim admitted himself to the emergency room due to the trauma of radiation. I assumed the worst, pain with a prognosis of death. When I walked into hospital room, he greeted me with a smile encouraging me. Jim demonstrated how much weight he lost by grabbing his arm and revealing his Harley tattoo. Once visible only on the outside of the arm, Jim lost so much weight the tattoo now wrapped all the way around his bicep, front and back. Then he said these words. "Soon I will die so I want to plan my funeral. Glen, it is good that you are a fisherman. The Lord caught me, now you get to release me." I felt as though I stood on holy ground. Pain and death had no hold on this man of deep faith. The vision of the holy stood taller and greater than his weakness and pain.

You go before me and follow me.
You place your hand of blessing on my head.
Such knowledge is too wonderful for me,
too great for me to understand!
Psalm 139.5-6

Now let's look at the next piece of the Lord's Prayer. *Your kingdom come, your will be done* form a transformational vision pointing to relationship with the Father doing His will. Before we look at this part of the prayer in detail let's examine a prayer dysfunction. Do you ever find prayer a self serving event? I mean to the point that perceived wants and needs overshadow His presence and will? Please allow me to use a graphic metaphor. I call these self centered requests parasitic prayers. A parasite lives on another organism usually causing harm. Sometimes I sense that I pray not for His fatherhood, but instead I use God to fix my life so I feel better. I did an internet search on parasitic treatments. Gross. But I did find an interesting word, encystment. This happens when an internal parasite encloses itself within a cyst in the muscles, liver, etc. In this state it multiplies, buds, forms spores. It is one thing to have a parasite floating in your digestive system or attaching itself to the intestinal wall. An entirely different ballgame results when the crazy little thing multiplies deep within the body. Did I say gross? Parasiticism drains energy. The host becomes symptomatic, but cannot feel where the infection festers. This is pretty tough stuff, but I think it a good picture of what takes place when prayer becomes serially about me.

Have you ever found yourself praying without transformation? I wonder if this defines parasitic prayers? I seek at times to drain the host of requests. Deep transformational prayer seeks the will of the Father. Look at the prayer of Jesus in the Garden of Gethsemane when he uses the intimate word for father, Abba.

He went on a little farther and fell to the ground. He prayed that, if it were possible, the awful hour awaiting might pass him by. "Abba, Father," He cried

*out, "everything is possible for you. Please take this cup of suffering away from
me. Yet I want your will to be done, not mine."*
Mark 14.35-36

Jesus wrestles. In one account forehead capillaries blow out and the Christ sweats drops of blood. Linger in His words. He addresses the Father with intimate words, Jesus affirms God's power, His honest desire to remove the cup of suffering, and then the resolution . . . to do the Father's will. I want you . . . your purpose . . . your plan . . . not mine. This is called the prayer of surrender. When I cross the line from feasting on the host, to surrendering my life and will over to the Father, barriers fall down. His presence and peace become power. The prayer for His kingdom cleanses me from parasitic petitions. I want the Father's plan within His kingdom community rather than my own host-draining desires.

An amazing result takes place, the power of connection with the Father. God is no host upon which to feed. He is the Father who loves and brings near.

Give us this day our daily bread.

I have often wondered if this part of the prayer has greater depth than asking for hotdogs, hamburgers, and hash browns. When we know God as Father, He fills the void of hunger for father. He touches the deepest aspect of our lives rewiring the mess, renewing us with honor, and bringing peace.

The word daily is an interesting Greek word meaning, "for the essence of life now." I think this prayer touches living in the moment of what is truly needed in life. This seems much richer than asking for details which God already knows like today's menu. Now, feel free to pray about what you will eat . . . that is ok. But let's take a step back and look at the whole prayer. The Lord's Prayer and the Great Prayer seek to transform us and we become whole in His presence. And let's face it sometimes I am not fully present in the moment are you? I find that I miss the significant nuances of life and can be quite dull. A man lay sprawled across three entire seats in a posh theater. When the usher came by and noticed this, he whispered to the man, "Sorry, sir, but you're only allowed one seat." The man groaned but didn't budge. The usher became impatient. "Sir, if you don't get up from there I'm going to have to call the manager." Again, the man just groaned, which infuriated the usher who turned and marched briskly back up the aisle in search of his manager. In a few moments, both the usher and the manager returned and stood over the man. Together the two of them tried repeatedly to move him, but with no success. Finally, they summoned the police. The cop surveyed the situation briefly then asked, "All right buddy, what's your name?" "Sam," the man moaned. "Where ya from, Sam?" With pain in his voice, Sam replied, "The balcony." Sometimes I hear myself praying on the perimeter of today's need. Not in tune with what truthfully takes place around me . . . I find oblivion and fog to be my friends.

Jesus asks me to pray for the fatherhood of God in reality of the moment. What is God's will right now for my family, my church, my own healing?

There is more to the picture of daily bread in the Lord's Prayer. Let's look at this passage painting a bigger picture of reality for the moment.

> *"I tell you the truth, anyone who believes has eternal life. Yes, I am the bread of life! Your ancestors ate manna in the wilderness, but they all died. Anyone who eats the bread from heaven, however, will never die. I am the living bread that came down from heaven. Anyone who eats this bread will live forever; and this bread, which I will offer so the world may live, is my flesh."*
> John 6.47

Jesus bakes the bread we need for today's reality, Himself. You have a spouse, a child, a friend, a family member who fell off the balcony. His presence of grace and love will save you, help you. In the Lord's Prayer when Jesus teaches us to pray for daily bread He urges us deeper into the fatherhood of God for the reality now.

> *Forgive us our debts, as we forgive our debtors.*

We now peer at the core of the prayer. Forgiveness frames the transformation of healing the heart. Steps 4-10 of the Twelve Steps of Alcoholics Anonymous say this;

4. Made a searching and fearless moral inventory of ourselves.
5. Admitted to God, to ourselves and to another human being the exact nature of our wrongs.
6. Were entirely ready to have God remove all these defects of character.
7. Humbly asked Him to remove our shortcomings.
8. Made a list of all persons we had harmed, and became willing to make amends to them all.
9. Made direct amends to such people wherever possible, except when to do so would injure them or others.
10. Continued to take personal inventory and when we were wrong promptly admitted it.

The majority of the twelve steps touch forgiveness. Look at steps 4-6. I examine myself, admit responsibility . . . and then humbly ask forgiveness. The word forgive means to send away or remove. The authors of the steps knew the Bible well and the core of the healing work of Jesus Christ. The cross of Christ stands as our icon of forgiveness. Jesus paid the penalty for sin and forgiveness is ours because of His sacrifice, and the result . . . we stand right with God. Steps 8-9 move forward from forgiving self to sending away the sin and brokenness of others. Step 9 is a powerful action step, *Made direct amends to such people wherever possible, except when to do so would injure them or others.* A young woman whose marriage I performed became disillusioned with her spouse and ended up in the arms of another man. She became pregnant by the illicit affair. I worked with diligence to help put the broken pieces back together. Faking a breakthrough the young woman claimed readiness to try the marriage again. I remember meeting with her and the spouse at a coffee shop. We discussed reconciliation. The next day a member of our church saw her with the other man and their baby walking along the beach. The marriage repair did not last. A year after her relationship with the lover failed, I received a letter from her. She expressed sorrow for the lies and betrayal. Healing begins with forgiveness.

Forgiveness frames the message of Jesus Christ. This forms the bedrock of our faith. Good God forgives broken mankind. A Polish preacher once said through an interpreter, "God never tires of forgiving." I have not forgotten those words. God never fatigues to send away sin and shame. Look at the psalmist's delight over forgiveness.

Psalm 103
Let all that I am praise the LORD;
with my whole heart, I will praise His holy name.
Let all that I am praise the LORD;
may I never forget the good things he does for me.
He forgives all my sins
and heals all my diseases.
He redeems me from death
and crowns me with love and tender mercies.
He fills my life with good things.
My youth is renewed like the eagle's!
The LORD gives righteousness
and justice to all who are treated unfairly.
He revealed His character to Moses
and His deeds to the people of Israel.
The LORD is compassionate and merciful,
slow to get angry and filled with unfailing love.
He will not constantly accuse us,
nor remain angry forever.
He does not punish us for all our sins;
He does not deal harshly with us, as we deserve.
For His unfailing love toward those who fear Him
is as great as the height of the heavens above the earth.
He has removed our sins as far from us
as the east is from the west.

The LORD is like a father to his children,
tender and compassionate to those who fear Him.
For He knows how weak we are;
He remembers we are only dust.

The fatherhood of God with compassion connects to the removing of sin and shame. No deeper prayer touches our hurt more profoundly than this one. Forgiveness is also serious business for deep relationships.

"If you forgive those who sin against you, your heavenly Father will forgive
you. But if you refuse to forgive others, your Father will not forgive your sins."
Matthew 6.14

When I choose to send away the right to get even . . . then the presence of God finds me. If I choose to refuse forgiveness, then His presence escapes me. Father hunger gnaws deeper when I do not forgive. I feel vacant because I am blank within.

Then Peter came to Him and asked, "Lord, how often should I forgive someone
who sins against me? Seven times? No, not seven times, Jesus replied, but
seventy times seven!"
Matthew 18. 21

Now Jesus instructs us to forgive without numeration. He desires no barrier between us and the Father. How many times do you forgive the bio dad who abused you? If we read this correctly in context, we forgive until the fatherhood of God replaces the emptiness of disappointment. A note however about forgiving, forgiveness does not allow trauma.

Then Peter came to Him and asked, "Lord, how often should I forgive someone
who sins against me? Seven times?"
"No, not seven times," Jesus replied, "but seventy times seven!
"Therefore, the Kingdom of Heaven can be compared to a king who decided
to bring his accounts up to date with servants who had borrowed money from
him. In the process, one of his debtors was brought in who owed him millions
of dollars. He couldn't pay, so his master ordered that he be sold–along with
his wife, his children, and everything he owned–to pay the debt.
"But the man fell down before his master and begged him, 'Please, be patient
with me, and I will pay it all.' Then his master was filled with pity for him,
and he released him and forgave his debt.

"But when the man left the king, he went to a fellow servant who owed him a few thousand dollars. He grabbed him by the throat and demanded instant payment.

"His fellow servant fell down before him and begged for a little more time. 'Be patient with me, and I will pay it,' he pleaded. But his creditor wouldn't wait. He had the man arrested and put in prison until the debt could be paid in full.

"When some of the other servants saw this, they were very upset. They went to the king and told him everything that had happened. Then the king called in the man he had forgiven and said, 'You evil servant! I forgave you that tremendous debt because you pleaded with me. Shouldn't you have mercy on your fellow servant, just as I had mercy on you?' Then the angry king sent the man to prison to be tortured until he had paid his entire debt.

"That's what my heavenly Father will do to you if you refuse to forgive your brothers and sisters from your heart."

Forgiving can be dangerous because it may open ourselves up for more trauma. Check out the story above. The king in this story does not allow the man to continue the trauma. God confronts abuse because his DNA is justice. In the passage below, again, you see the heart of God to confront and correct.

"If another believer sins against you, go privately and point out the offense. If the other person listens and confesses it, you have won that person back. But if you are unsuccessful, take one or two others with you and go back again, so that everything you say may be confirmed by two or three witnesses. If the person still refuses to listen, take your case to the church. Then if he or she won't accept the church's decision, treat that person as a pagan or a corrupt tax collector.
Matthew 18. 15

Paul the Apostle speaks of confronting as well. Godly people according to Paul face sin with gentleness and humility. The words in Galatians 6.1-2 *help that person back onto the right path* in the Greek language mean to "triage". I also like his admonition to be careful not to project our personal problems onto others. He calls this kind of confrontation, sharing in other's pain. When we engage this, we honor or obey the law of Christ.

Dear brothers and sisters, if another believer is overcome by some sin, you who are godly should gently and humbly help that person back onto the right path. And be careful not to fall into the same temptation yourself. Share each other's burdens, and in this way obey the law of Christ.
Galatians 6.1-2

When you look at the passion of Jesus to forgive, you also see a deep concern for confrontation of sin and abuse. Because we forgive we do not open the door to ongoing trauma, but rather truth.

Forgiveness forms the core of the Lord's Prayer and the center of the recovery movements today. Forgiveness opens the door to the fatherhood of God. The next piece of the Lord's Prayer says,

> *Don't let us yield to temptation, but rescue us from the evil one.*

Jesus wants us to pray about not giving into temptation. Another note on anxiety: a synonym for the word group temptation, test, and trial includes the word anxiety. Jesus challenges us to be fully present when we feel tempted which can undermine faith in God. Let's look at temptation and the transformation of prayer when temptation grips us.

> *Then Jesus, full of the Holy Spirit, returned from the Jordan River. He was led*
> *by the Spirit in the wilderness, . . .*
> *Luke 4:1*

Full of the Spirit Jesus experienced an amazing fatherhood moment with the verbal affirmation of the Father for the Son, and now divine guidance leads him into a storm of temptation. May I encourage you as you learn to pray? God designs temptation to send you deeper spiritually, to depend on the fatherhood of God more richly. Temptation is not the final word in your life. The Father's intent is not punishment, but rather the Spirit leads you to the presence of God.

> *When the devil had finished tempting Jesus,*
> *he left Him until the next opportunity came.*
> *Luke 4:13*

With every temptation comes an end to the anxiety. When worry racks you, God's control still endures. He goes to amazing lengths to send you deeper spiritually. Look with me.

> *Simon, Simon, Satan has asked to test all of you as a farmer sifts his wheat. I*
> *have prayed that you will not lose your faith! Help your brothers be stronger*
> *when you come back to me."*
> *Luke 22. 31-32*

Temptation and events of anxiety happen so that we do not lose faith in the Father and so we can help others grow stronger. God also uses temptation events to help grow through pride.

To keep me from becoming conceited because of these surpassingly great revelations there was given me a thorn in my flesh a messenger from Satan to torment me.
2 Cor. 12.7

This is a good thing. Humility opens the door to healing. Pride slams the door shut.

Three times I pleaded with the Lord to take it away from me. But he said to me, "My grace is sufficient for you, my power is made perfect in weakness."
2 Cor. 12.8

God still controls. His grace is enough. The point and power of prayer is this, prayer connects you to Him and Christ is all you need to heal.

Finally, temptation and trials complete the rewiring. A violent act in the book of Genesis tore Joseph from his father. Joseph lost honor, presence, and fatherhood in one day. Joseph in the book of Genesis was abused by his brothers. They faked his death and sold him into slavery telling his dad that he died a violent death in the teeth of wild animals. A blood soaked coat proved their deception. Joseph went through hard trials, temptation, and he endured. He hungered for his father, but in his anxiety and loss kept looking for the perfect Father. Numerous times in the story of his life the words emerge, and *"God was with Joseph."* God blessed Joseph promoting him through the ranks and he becomes the CFO of Egypt, second only to the President. During an intense recession his abusive brothers travel to Egypt for an agricultural stimulas bail out in a troubled economy. Joseph stands face to face with the men who caused him a lifetime of heartbreak, separation from family, and torture. What would you do? When I am wronged, I imagine martial arts and round house kicks for my adversaries. Listen to the powerful words of forgiveness,

What you intended for evil, God meant it for good.
Genesis 50.20

What the evil one intends for evil God purposes for good. God controls. Purpose exists for your pain. He wastes nothing when it comes to the healing of your heart.

Jesus knows your hardwiring. He understands that you have weaknesses, anxiety, and trials. Look at His words.

Keep watch and pray, so that you will not give in to temptation. For the spirit is willing, but the body is weak!"
Matthew 26:41

You will be tempted to use and to despair. I am. This prayer invites all that God is into your pain. He controls. Not you . . . not me. Evil is not in control . . . therefore you will be ok when the anxiety of trials grip you. Choose Him. He never tires of forgiving. The perfect parent stands with you.

The final sentence of the Lord's Prayer speaks to power and connects us with presence and honor (glory) once again.

You are the kingdom, power, and glory forever.

When you live on the coast, storm management becomes second nature. We had a big one not long ago. Two days of sustained winds over 60 mph with gusts over 100 pounded our community. Millions of board feet of trees fell. Stands of forests snapped half way up the tree . . . looked like an atomic bomb blast. Trees toppled in crisscross patterns blocking roads making them impassable for days. The greatest traumas? No communication with the outside world and no power for the inside world. We could not call out to loved ones because the cell towers possessed no power. We lived by candle light for 4 days. Idealistic for an evening maybe, but after 4 dark nights we felt exhausted and quite unromantic.

Driving through the county surveying damage, we noticed hundreds of trees pushed onto their sides exposing shallow root systems. Hundreds. I called a tree expert friend of mine and he said that because of prolific coastal rain, the trees don't need to send roots deep. They receive the nutrition they need by skimming off the surface. Where we live is most often paradise . . . lovely weather with stunning coastal panoramas. In paradise roots don't need depth. All you require rests on the surface. Why grow deeper if you can skim what you need off the surface?

We also saw trees that stood tall in the storm. They endured the same 100 mph winds, but still stand strong. For some reason their roots went deep before the storm and held fast when the world tried to blow them away.

For the better part of a week we watched a community in hot pursuit of connection and power. Hundreds of anxious storm victims stood in long lines waiting to fill empty gas cans fueling overheated generators to cool melting meals. Strangers asked strangers the number one question, "Did you get power yet?" We were a coastal community fixated with communicating and power. I recall looking into the faces of people without light. They seemed so empty, lost, looking for hope or a glimmer in the cold darkness. I wonder if the intense focus on power unmasked self reliance. Anxieties grow when I can no longer flip a wall switch and control sight with light.

Jesus teaches us to pray for kingdom and the power of His presence. I think he asks us to pray for deep roots before storms. Storms of relapse, finances, marriage, singleness loom building intensity and pressure. When they strike, it's too late to go deep. You take into the explosion of wind and rain the spirituality you possess.

Kingdom community and the power of His presence sink deep spiritual roots through prayer.

People who make it through the healing of their hearts send down deep roots before storms. Here is a simple formula; shallow equals poor results. Deep spirituality produces power. If your roots grow deep and you surround yourselves with others of depth, you will make it through the blast just fine.

Let's take an up close look at an Old Testament storm. Job's life melted down. He lost his wealth. His family died in a desert storm. His health hit the skids. Job cursed his birthday. Ask Him, Job would tell you his life reeked. He lost everything. Or did he? Look at his words after the storm surge.

> *I know that you can do anything and no one can stop you . . . I had heard*
> *about you before, but now I have seen you with my own eyes.*
> *Job 42. 2-5 NLT*

Job survives the thrashing. On the other side of suffering immense loss Job prays and affirms God's power. Job says that before the typhoon he understood God only with ears, but afterward his knowledge touched the depth of experience. The wonder of prayer is depth, power, and perspective in the storms. God controls. I am small. He is big. Storms reveal the depth of spirituality. Squalls give you a GPS position on your recovery.

How deep are you when winds blow 90 mph? When your roof blows off, does your temper go with it? In the anxiety of the storm do you drink and drug? Do you allow your hurt to hammer your family?

Prayer is the only way to grow deeper before the storm . . . nothing else will work for you. Fair weather follower, did you go through a storm and feel surprised by what came out of you? Go deeper now.

The Book of Revelation predicts a violent cataclysm from falling stars, plagues, to persecution this book foretells a terrible tempest. Then those with deep roots, who loved Him, find treasure. In the final chapter of Revelation victims of eschatological rage receive kingdom, power, presence; the person of Christ.

> *Then I saw a new heaven and a new earth, for the old heaven and the*
> *old earth had disappeared. And the sea was also gone. And I saw the holy*
> *city, the new Jerusalem, coming down from God out of heaven like a bride*
> *beautifully dressed for her husband.*
> *I heard a loud shout from the throne, saying, "Look, God's home is now among*
> *His people! He will live with them, and they will be His people. God Himself*
> *will be with them, He will wipe every tear from their eyes, and there will be*
> *no more death or sorrow or crying or pain. All these things are gone forever."*
> *And the one sitting on the throne said, "Look, I am making everything new!"*
> *And then he said to me, "Write this down, for what I tell you is trustworthy*

and true." And he also said, "It is finished! I am the Alpha and the Omega–the Beginning and the End. To all who are thirsty I will give freely from the springs of the water of life. All who are victorious will inherit all these blessings, and I will be their God, and they will be my children.

You have a storm of cancer, that is bad, but God is good. Your shingles blew off, that's a bummer, but God brings near. You relapsed. You criticized. You feel overwhelming temptation to leave, to betray your vows . . . God stands near. Instead of asking Him to change your spouse, ask the Father to rewire you . . . His spirit to move you. Speak to Him . . . listen . . . grow deep. Do you find your prayers asking for more stuff, using prayer as one more means to mask and medicate pain? Ask for Him. He loves to answer that prayer. Prayer deepens roots before the storm.

Kingdom, power, glory. Praying His fatherhood heals. He is what you need. In this intimate relationship you get Him. Prayer is a treasure. Treasure is power. Treasure is Christ. You change.

Paul the Apostle writes an inspired equation for healing the hurt of our lives. Worry launches addiction and as well the rage and denial of abusers. Prayer invites the peace of God into anxious neurology. The Father guards the heart and mind. His powerful presence embraces when you pray. Addiction loosens its grip. The disempowerment of survivors finds connection with Christ. Look at Paul's equation for healing in Philippians 4.

Don't worry about anything; instead, pray about everything. Tell God what you need, and thank Him for all he has done. Then you will experience God's peace, which exceeds anything we can understand. His peace will guard your hearts and minds as you live in Christ Jesus.
And now, dear brothers and sisters, one final thing. Fix your thoughts on what is true, and honorable, and right, and pure, and lovely, and admirable. Think about things that are excellent and worthy of praise. Keep putting into practice all you learned and received from me–everything you heard from me and saw me doing. Then the God of peace will be with you.
Philippians 4 NLT

He will be with you. Choose Christ before the storm. You get His presence beyond understanding. Moses writes in Deuteronomy 4.7 *"What other nation is so great as to have their gods near them the way the Lord our God is near us whenever we pray to Him?"* Peace replaces anxiety. Subtle shifts in neurons take place. Balance restores. The trauma passes and peace finds you.

We have spent a tremendous time on prayer. Prayer is the path to know the One who cares. You must go beyond theory and acquisition of data to heal your pain. Prayer connects to the healer. Talking to your Father rewires the family mess in your mind. Listening renews. Nearness to the presence of God rescripts the broken images of the Father and oneness emerges. Our addiction and trauma launches aloneness. Prayer reconnects. You never weep alone. Pray for His presence and healing happens. When your heart is heavy, no soul in sight to help, you feel desperate, He speaks the word that heals. The Father loves you.

I put this chapter in the center of the book because of its value to you. Healing your hurt does not work in the ethereal. Theories, steps, and strategies have no power unless you engage. This is your time to heal. Ask Him. Recovery from the hurt of your heart is no game. It is your life, your family, your marriage, your singleness. Grow deep. Prayer blazes the way. When I read leading books on addiction and trauma, I feel as though the authors look at us from the outside. Prayer brings the reality of transformation into our world. You can know it now. Prayer is the special place where the Father and the child meet . . . healing takes place here. Ask.

Below is the rest of Niebuhr's prayer. Look at the depth of love and presence of the Father.

Living one day at a time;
Enjoying one moment at a time;
Accepting hardships as the pathway to peace;
Taking, as He did, this sinful world
as it is, not as I would have it;
Trusting that He will make all things right if I surrender to His Will;
That I may be reasonably happy in this life and supremely happy with Him
Forever in the next.
Amen.–Reinhold Niebuhr

Father hunger gnaws the human spirit. The fourth horseman of anxiety launches addiction and idolatry. The Lord's Prayer begins with Father. Rewiring begins. You start to connect with the One who loves you best. He has never failed you. God makes His heart your home. He created you for this. Holy takes us deeper to transformation. Kingdom community frames the place and people where rescripting the fatherhood of God begins. His will begins to take the place of the narcissism of addiction and trauma. Daily bread is the reality we need. Forgiveness removes the barriers for the perfect parent to take residence in our lives. Bitterness and resentment keep Him out. Temptation opens doors to depth. The evil one substitutes the shallowness of obsessions and compulsions for His presence. Kingdom, power, glory cast the vision of the Father satiating the deepest of all hungers . . . the need for Him.

Perhaps we have stepped into the greatest healing grace in human history. Prayer fills the innate need for Father. We have seen the Lord's Prayer as liturgy, cool devotional material, but never as the door to fill the deepest need and longing of the human heart. This path for millions today cures addictions, idolatries, marriages, singleness, eating disorders . . . the Father fills through prayer.

Great hope emerges here. You had an absent or crummy dad? The loss and angst can drive you into the arms of the perfect Father. Let go of past hurts and run to Him. He loves you, he cares. The Father cannot hurt you. Great power unearths at this point. Healing happens from deep within and peace replaces craziness.

You can experience the fatherhood of God in a small group community among praying people who have been rewired, renewed, and reparented by the perfect Father. You will experience the encouragement of friends. Call, God answers. He cares. The Father watches like an eagle when you despair. He loves without condition. You may not be the person you want to become, but you are not the person you once were. You may be a mess, but you are His mess. You belong to the Father.

Small Group Bible Study

I trust you are having a great experience in your small group. Are you connecting, enjoying one another? Prayer is so important for a small group community. Can you pray that you will each grow deeply as you learn to forgive?

Let's look at some passages about forgiveness. This study is very special. We will pray together and seek forgiveness.

> *"If you forgive those who sin against you, your heavenly Father will forgive you. 15 But if you refuse to forgive others, your Father will not forgive your sins.*
> *Matthew 6.14*

> *Then Peter came to Him and asked, "Lord, how often should I forgive someone who sins against me? Seven times?" "No, not seven times," Jesus replied, "but seventy times seven!*
> *Matthew 18. 21*

> *Dear brothers and sisters, if another believer is overcome by some sin, you who are godly should gently and humbly help that person back onto the right path. And be careful not to fall into the same temptation yourself. Share each other's burdens, and in this way obey the law of Christ.*
> *Galatians 6.1-2*

1. When you read these passages do so in several translations ok? You will like the nuances. Is forgiving serious? Why?

2. Describe how we prevent trauma, what is the character we take with us in Matthew 18?

3. How can you prevent abuse based on Galatians 6.1-2?

This is a very special story written by a mentor of mine, perhaps one of the greatest stories of forgiveness I have ever heard. Enjoy this and reflect deeply on the fatherhood of God and forgiveness.

Forrest's Story

Our orders in August 1969 were to lay down recon fire 100 meters outside a Vietnamese village to drive out the inhabitants and then disperse CS, powdered tear gas. CS would make this lethal enemy outpost uninhabitable for at least a year and save many lives. 9 of my buddies and I walked toward the village in a straight line, 4 on my left and 5 on my right, some 15 meters apart. Without realizing we stepped over 3 well concealed Viet Cong bunkers in a dry rice patty. We stopped at the 100 meter mark to begin laying down fire. As I knelt steadying the M16 with my right elbow on my right thigh, I suddenly noticed 30 caliber and AK47 machine gun rounds kicking up the dark earth around me. Grabbing my radio to call in a gun ship I found myself knocked to the ground staring into the humid blue sky. Quickly inventorying my body I counted one right boot, but no left. The popping sounds to the right drew my immediate attention to 3 North Vietnamese Army Regulars (NVA) executing my wounded comrades. The M16 I carried landed beyond my grasp when I was hit . . . I could not move to retrieve the weapon because my missing left ankle lodged securely beneath my head. The return fire to my left came from our wounded platoon lieutenant crawling toward me. When the LT was hit, I used his weapon to defend myself until help arrived. I only survived.

After the war, I married my beautiful wife Pamela. It soon became evident that getting pregnant wasn't going to be easy for us. We were both disappointed, but Pamela was especially distressed by it. She longed to be a mother with every fiber of her being. We visited the doctor without result. I suppose we could have taken heroic steps with a fertilization clinic, but Pam developed a vision for adopting a little girl from China. We started developing the dossier required for a China adoption. It turned out to be a complex and daunting task. So we began a passionate life of prayer for our adopted child.

I remember the day we presented our dossier to the adoption agency. We were very excited. Two weeks later, we got a call. Our contact explained that China had changed some rules and wouldn't allow adoptions to parents who were more than 30 years older than the adoptive child. That new rule disqualified us both. That essentially killed our prospects in China. We were floored, not to mention distraught. Our contact told us we had other options and not to lose hope. We had been entirely focused on China and hadn't considered anything else. The good news was that the dossier we'd constructed for China was more than adequate for other countries with a few small changes. We considered adopting from Russia, Thailand, India, Columbia, Eastern Europe, and Vietnam.

I had been a combat soldier in Vietnam during 1968 and 1969. I was wounded at the end of my tour and had spent several years in a hospital and in a wheel chair. In spite of extensive veteran counseling and an understanding of the importance of forgiveness, I could not imagine adopting a child from Vietnam. I realized, to my surprise, that I still had some unresolved issues. I tried not to let Pamela know, but she could tell I was having trouble with the idea.

We drove home from the agency and I escaped into a book I was reading at the time. It was a novel by Randy Alcorn called *Deadline*. I opened it up and almost immediately read, "When you go to war with a people, you dehumanize them to do what you do in war. If you ever expect to reconcile with that people, you have to consciously promote them back to humanity." I was stunned. It was like God was speaking directly to me through that passage. I shared what I'd read with Pamela. I asked her to give me a few days to work through my feelings. She was gracious to me. I prayed diligently, but also searched hard for a way out. I wrestled with the idea of going to Vietnam. I struggled over working with the Communists. I tried to imagine being the father of a little Vietnamese child whose grandparents tried to kill me. Once I told Pamela that going to Vietnam would be OK, she was on the phone to the agency before I could turn around. It took about a week for my emotions to catch up with my declarations and what I knew was right. But they did, pretty much.

It didn't take long for my precarious conviction to be tested. We got a call from the agency a few weeks later. They had wonderful news. We actually had an opportunity to adopt twin boys. It would be a while before I felt right about it, but I knew I would. I just stuffed it and followed Pamela's lead. She knew my heart and trusted me.

We got a picture of the boys a few days later. They were 10 weeks old and each weighed three pounds. They were clearly malnourished, but they had all their limbs and looked beautiful to Pamela. They looked scary to me. We were told they were in an orphanage in a southern province called Tra Vinh, near the Mekong Delta.

The boys' names were Dam and Dang. That gave us pause. Perhaps the names Joshua and Benjamin would serve them better as they grew up in the U.S. Joshua was a name we both loved and had talked about for years. We began to pray for the boys and as the weeks and months dragged by, we took them into our hearts and they became our own. They became our sons.

On our 6th wedding anniversary we got a call that Dam, our Joshua, had died. We were profoundly shaken by the news. They assured us that Benjamin was healthy and we should still plan on making the trip to Vietnam. We could hardly wait. We were anxious to hold our son in our arms. Once again prayer became our connection with God.

Our agency liaison, Hung, met us at airport in Saigon (Ho Chi Minh City) and took us to our hotel. Neither Pamela nor I were prepared for navigating our way in a Third World Country.

On our fourth day, we were scheduled for a very early drive to Tra Vinh. We would meet Benjamin for the first time and participate in the Giving and Receiving Ceremony. Through that, he would legally become our son.

After a chilling ferry ride across the Mekong Delta, and a little over 8 hours after leaving Saigon, we pulled into Tra Vinh, the capital of Tra Vinh Province. Hung drove out of town and turned onto a narrow path that we expected would lead to the orphanage. We were excited, but after almost an hour on that path our excitement turned to anxiety. The country side had become jungle and our surroundings became more and more familiar to me and my combat experience. It was like a flashback. We finally drove into a small compound of three buildings, one that was about 3,000 square feet, and two smaller structures. We were ushered into the smallest. It was essentially a meeting room with a large table and about 20 chairs surrounded by four thin walls. Hung told us to wait there and he would be, "back in few minutes."

Forty-five minutes later, we were frantic. Something had to be wrong. I assured Pam that they were not being controlling, disrespectful, or mean spirited. I didn't tell her I knew it was very difficult for people in Eastern cultures to deliver bad news. Hung finally returned and said there had been some complications. The Director of the orphanage would see us soon. Soon was another 30 minutes. The Director came in and introduced himself through Hung. Hung's English had been pretty difficult to understand up to that point, but manageable. Now that we needed to really understand what was going on, the language barrier became particularly inconvenient. The bottom line seemed to be that Benjamin was sick and had been taken to the hospital a few days earlier. The Director suggested we go home and try to adopt another baby some day. That was not OK. I turned to Hung and asked him if he knew where the hospital was. To Hung's credit, he discovered the hospital location from the Director in a rather heated exchange.

As we stepped into the Children's Ward, Hung spotted someone in a white coat and headed for him. We were stunned by what we saw. The room was probably 20 by 30 feet and crowded wall to wall with baby cribs. There seemed to be 2 or 3 children in every crib. Hung pointed to one about a third of the way into the room. It held a tiny infant and a little 2 year old boy. We moved through a sea of cribs to get to it. Both children were tied down, but the larger boy had gotten a foot loose and was thrashing in agony. His leg was inadvertently landing on the infant and I cringed every time it came down. The infant seemed too sick to complain. Hung motioned to the infant and told us he was Benjamin. My knees went weak. Pam leaned against me and started to sink. It was all I could do to hold her up. Ben was so tiny. He looked so sick. There were open soars all over his little body and he had a plastic oxygen tube taped to his little face. He could not possibly be seven months old. He didn't look like he weighed more than 5 pounds. As I took a closer look at the larger boy, I realized he must be more like six, maybe seven years old.

Pamela and I stepped out into the hall with Hung only to be jostled and scrutinized by scores and scores of people who were either sick or visiting the sick, and all highly curious about us. Standing in that hall the walls seemed to get closer somehow. I shook myself and knew that we needed more help. So we prayed.

It felt like every circumstance was conspiring to defeat us. I couldn't even think in all the press of bodies, the noise, and intense scrutiny we were under in that hall outside Benjamin's ward. There were at least 80 children in that room, some crying and screaming, and some too sick to even moan. There was a single doctor, if indeed that's what he was, caring for them. It was one of the most heartbreaking experiences I have ever had. I felt completely helpless. So, we prayed again.

Soon the hospital released Ben without complaint and we visited the People's Committee building in Tra Vinh to finalize Benjamin's adoption before we could leave for Saigon.

At the People's Committee Building, there was a bunch of paperwork and the formal Giving Receiving Ceremony. It would take well over an hour.

Finally, the paperwork was ready. About a dozen government workers were invited into the room and I was offered a warm glass of beer. Pamela got a glass of soda. We were expected to take at least a sip. Everyone in the room seemed frozen until we each did just that. They asked us to sit at a table with the Director. Finally, we were done signing and it was the Director's turn.

The Director was probably 60 years old. He took his time and looked at each of us for a long moment. He then reached into his coat. As he pulled a gold pen from his pocket and unscrewed the cap, he looked at me hard and finally said in English, "You in American War, Yes?" I had never heard the Vietnam War called the American War, but I knew what he meant. I froze. Our eyes locked. I wanted to lie. We both knew then that we had been mortal enemies 30 years earlier. I looked him in the eye and decided to be as straight as possible. I gave him the friendliest, most empathetic smile I could muster and said, "Yes, I was." He looked back at me with a life time of experience scrolling behind his inscrutable expression. I felt a chill. 30 years earlier I faced a Viet Cong with a white knuckle grip on my rifle, today I stared down an NVA Regular holding only my beautiful Benjamin in gentle embrace. At last, the former enemy gave me a small nod, signed all the documents without another word and left the room.

The Vietnamese people were once my enemy. I had adopted someone who was once my enemy and it was one of the greatest things God had ever allowed me to do. In Benjamin, I had not only reconciled myself to these people, I had made a covenant with him to be his father for as long as we both existed. An adoption is not a contract, conditional on each party keeping its terms. Adoption is instead a sacred covenant and is, by definition, an unconditional commitment. No matter what, Benjamin will always know that I chose to be his father and I will always love him and care for him without condition.

I clearly understood that I was once God's enemy. At some point in my life, I discovered that Jesus had made a way for me to be reconciled to Him. It occurred to me that reconciliation included His adoption of me into His family. He is my heavenly Father. He will never leave me nor forsake me. That's a reconciliation and adoption that is an eternal covenant, the most important relationship in the history of man. And, God had allowed me to experience that covenant as an adoptive father, as well as His adopted son. What a gracious Father He is.

Writing Your Story, Healing Your Heart

Write out the names of the people who hurt you. You may use initials. What is the consequence of their actions? What do you need forgiveness for? What are the results of your sin? Take a few minutes and write out your story of forgiveness. Share your story with your group. Have communion together. Bring Kleenex.

1. The people who hurt you:

2. The consequences:

3. What do you need forgiveness for? Whom did you hurt?

4. Write out a prayer for forgiveness. Include the people who hurt you and then write out your prayer for personal forgiveness.

Heroes

I HAVE HAD the privilege of being mentored by exceptional teachers over my career. From my undergraduate studies through my doctoral program wise mentors invested themselves in my life and ministry. At Asbury College it was Dr. Gerald Miller, a brilliant linguist. His commitment to faith and reason still inspire me living in my head daily. Dr. David Turner of Grand Rapids Theological Seminary helped me discover the riches of Paul's writings on grace and community. Dr. Tom Boogaart of Western Seminary touched me with his transparency, humility, and love for the Scriptures. Wendy Collins, an amazing evangelist, and C.D. Boiley, former CEO of Hills Brother's Coffee walked me through Christlike leadership truths. As I have served post modern people with chemical and non substance relational attachments, another significant mentor has risen to guide me through the deeper issues of addiction and trauma. To honor confidentiality I will change his name and tell his story in twelve step parabolic form. I call my mentor, Shorty.

"Hi, my name is Shorty. My hang up is process addiction, non substance attachment to control and rage." The group responds, "Hi Shorty." "I manipulate and rage when I cannot control. I grew up in an ultra religious home. My parents held firm convictions. Dedicated to God as an infant, I enjoyed private religious education and I studied the Bible with excellence. I memorized it, carried it, loved it. When old enough to choose, I became a minister of the word teaching the Bible's tenets with an iron grip, inflexible in application.

I came on too strong. Frankly, I made others afraid of me. I carried people away with my passion. My strong views when opposed became rage. Fury fired to the point of violence when others disagreed with me.

Envy robs me of peace. I watched with great interest Christians who faced disaster with grace. They were relaxed, had it together, I didn't get it. Had to be flawless and demand others be so as well. I felt anxious about the fact that Christians lived by a deeper and richer-treasure than a performance driven plan. I lived lost and incomplete with my list of rules.

The external need to manipulate others projected deeper truth about me. Inner control constrained me. As close to religion and the speech of God as a person can be, I possessed no personal transforming vision of a God who loved me and would give his heart for me. I hurt good people. I sought opportunities to put down kind Christians who lived out their faith. In such deep denial, I could not see my own sin and shame. A walking wrecking ball of relationships, addictive thinking incarcerated me. This striking-out projected my own guilt and shame of imperfection, locked in a system of personal performance and control. My thinking distorted. Trying to describe grace and the love of God was like asking a blind man for directions. Amazing, to be so close to Christianity, but far from Christ.

I still wrestle with shame and self loathing. Despicable is a good adjective. I feel grief stricken living in this shell. I am not perfect inside. I hate being out of control. I don't comprehend why I engage the thinking and behavior I do. A sinful truth raises its ugly head in me. It's all out war at times. I feel more like a POW than a pastor. I want to do right, but "a something" in my neurology messes me up. I feel frustrated. I fight. I argue with God.

The treasure for me unearthed on a roadway of rage, a path of my own brokenness. Christ found me. He gave gifts of grace-not guilt. His kindness, tenderness with my sin and shame seemed like sight to a blind man. I thought I could earn my way to heaven, please God through performing, but in His presence I drank in forgiveness and acceptance. He called me to be a pastor leading the very people I loathed.

Now I sense peace. I feel as though a concentration camp couldn't steal this grace from me. I am not so hung up on my perfection, as I am His. He set me free from the anxiety of performance oriented religion. I controlled people, dragged them out of the sphere of choice and imposed my systems of belief on them. I stepped over boundaries, chose not to allow others to be or do according to their conscience. Inner rage drove me. A gentle savior tenderly placed this wrath on Himself at the cross. He is my peace.

A new system controls now. I have the power to give and receive love, feel joy, I am no serial worrier, my friends tell me that a tenderness, a gentleness fills my words. I belong to Christ. I gladly nail myself to His grace rather than attach to the narcissistic need for manipulation. I feel a calling; I hear a voice of love and invitation. The power of this transformation is stunning.

The freedom from addictive thinking I have found reflects not my resume, but rather the grace of God in Jesus Christ. He creates in me His goodness and strength. His peace recreates my broken neurology. He brings balance to my anxiety and shame. And, I will pass with that." The group responds, "Thanks, pastor."

Shorty's last name was "of Tarsus". His pious friends called him Saul. His epistolary pen name, Paul. He was the greatest missionary of first century Christianity. His Spirit inspired words have transformed kings and kingdoms, Czars and Caesars. Paul's words on grace changed my life.

Paul can be described in a number of ways. He is known as the premier theologian of the New Testament. Paul's writings inspired Luther and began a revolution built on grace through faith. Evangelists have used the Pauline Romans' Road to lead millions to faith in Christ. Some consider him a mystic. He had deep spiritual experiences with Christ. The community of faith in which I serve views Paul as a mentor teaching addicts how to recover. His words of grace bring hope and healing to addicted traumatized lives. The recovery circles of our church see Paul as a fellow addict who found wholeness in Jesus Christ for non-substance addictions of rage and control. When our recovery groups read the twelve steps, they also cite the biblical comparisons. The first step of twelve reads, "We admitted we were powerless over our addictions and compulsive behaviors, that our lives had become unmanageable." The biblical comparison comes from Paul's autobiography in Romans 7.18, "*I know that nothing good lives in me, that is, in my sinful nature. For I have the desire to do what is good, but I cannot carry it out*" *Romans 7.17-18(NIV)* (Baker, p. 11). Paul inspires addicts and survivors to continue in the healing grace of Jesus Christ. Addicts find their own story in the testimony of Paul.

When I first heard my addict friends speak of Paul in this manner, frankly I felt offense. How can they attach the stigma of addiction to such a great icon of our faith? Doesn't that diminish his stature? So, in order to have a deeper understanding of their perspective I researched criteria of addiction and related them to Paul's biblical witness. Dr. Gerald May states that addiction involves a three step process: feelings of pleasure or gratification attached to an activity, a choice to repeat the behavior, and loss of restraint (May, pp. 57-60). May also gives several key characteristics of addiction: tolerance, the presence of anxious-irritable behaviors, self deception, powerlessness to overcome attachment behavior, and the inability to love (May, pp. 26-29). Let's examine the historical record and put Paul's non-substance attachment to rage and control to the test.

The Stoning of Stephen
When they heard this, they were furious and gnashed their teeth at him. But Stephen, full of the Holy Spirit, looked up to heaven and saw the glory of God, and Jesus standing at the right hand of God. "Look," he said, "I see heaven open and the Son of Man standing at the right hand of God."
At this they covered their ears and, yelling at the top of their voices, they all rushed at him, dragged him out of the city and began to stone him. Meanwhile, the witnesses laid their clothes at the feet of a young man named Saul.

> *While they were stoning him, Stephen prayed, "Lord Jesus, receive my spirit."*
> *Then he fell on his knees and cried out, "Lord, do not hold this sin against*
> *them." When he had said this, he fell asleep.*
> *And Saul was there, giving approval to his death.*
> *On that day a great persecution broke out against the church at Jerusalem,*
> *and all except the apostles were scattered throughout Judea and Samaria.*
> *Godly men buried Stephen and mourned deeply for him. But Saul began to*
> *destroy the church. Going from house to house, he dragged off men and women*
> *and put them in prison. Acts 7.54-8.3 NIV*

In the Acts passage Luke uses a statement indicating a sense of pleasure as Paul persecutes the embryonic church. Luke uses the term "giving approval" (well pleased with) to the murder of Stephen (Scott, p. 676). It seems Paul enjoyed his persecution of the church. Galatians 1 gives another pleasure perception. Paul states that he "did his best" (meaning to outdo, excel, surpass) to attack Christians with violence (Scott, p. 731).

> *You know what I was like when I followed the Jewish religion-how I violently*
> *persecuted the Christians. I did my best to get rid of them. I was one of the*
> *most religious Jews of my own age, and I tried as hard as possible to follow all*
> *the old traditions of my religion. But then something happened! For it pleased*
> *God in His kindness to choose me and call me, even before I was born! What*
> *undeserved mercy! Then he revealed His Son to me so that I could proclaim the*
> *Good News about Jesus to the Gentiles.*
> *Galatians 1.13-16 NLT*

When I look at these words, I get the impression that more than a professional terrorist, he liked what he did. On the eve of Paul's conversion in Acts 9, the historical record states that he was "*still breathing out threats*" repeating the rage filled thinking (1). If terrorism includes the characteristic of irritability, then Paul had this too. In his Romans 7 autobiography Paul speaks of an inner loss of control as he engages a personal wrestling match with evil. "*For what I do is not the good I want to do; no, the evil I do not want to do–this I keep on doing. Now if I do what I do not want to do, it is no longer I who do it, but it is sin living in me that does it*" *(Romans 7:15-17 NIV)*. I call his inner conflict "war at the neuron level." Self deception and inability to love unearth in the witnessing of Stephen's stoning. The future Apostle stood stoically as his colleagues brutally murdered a gentle man of God filled with the Spirit of Christ. While the jury still deliberates on tolerance, I think the recovery community is astute to identify addiction language and attachment characteristics in Paul's autobiography.

Although the stigma of labeling Paul still does not set well with me, I see a deeper issue. Addicts and survivors have a mentor; someone with deep theological integrity, a transparent hero who believed dying for Jesus was as rich a treasure as living for Him, a broken Apostle who found grace at the cross, and power over his attachments through Christ's resurrection.

Paul is my hero. He is theologian, missionary, mystic, and now a post modern mentor for wounded hearts seeking a deeper richer life.

Small Group Bible Study

Reconnect with your group, highlights and lowlights. Start with prayer, share your story of forgiveness from last week if you wish. Now, let's look at this passage from the chapter.

> *"For what I do is not the good I want to do; no, the evil I do not want to do–this I keep on doing. Now if I do what I do not want to do, it is no longer I who do it, but it is sin living in me that does it"*
> *Romans 7:15-17 NIV*

1. Paul is an amazing mentor. Look at his story. He struggles. How does Paul's story of struggle help you and inspire you?

2. Here is another powerful statement. Paul makes quite an admission. Again, how does this mentoring help you?

> *So I find this law at work: When I want to do good, evil is right there with me. For in my inner being I delight in God's law; but I see another law at work in the members of my body, waging war against the law of my mind and making me a prisoner of the law of sin at work within my members. What a wretched man I am! Who will rescue me from this body of death? Thanks be to God–through Jesus Christ our Lord! Romans 7.21-25 (NIV)*

3. Now just when you think this faith journey is too hard, look at Romans 8. Discuss with your group the hope you see.

> *Therefore, there is now no condemnation for those who are in Christ Jesus, because through Christ Jesus the law of the Spirit of life set me free from the law of sin and death. For what the law was powerless to do in that it was weakened by the sinful nature, God did by sending His own Son in the likeness of sinful man to be a sin offering. And so He condemned sin in sinful man, in order that the righteous requirements of the law might be fully met in us, who do not live according to the sinful nature but according to the Spirit.*
> *Romans 8.1-3 (NIV)*

Writing Your Story, Healing Your Heart

Who are the people who have helped you on the way? Mention the significant people the Lord has put in your life. Whom are you mentoring to encourage toward life transformation? Write your mentoring story below. Send your mentors a thank you note, Facebook them, I bet you a dollar they could use some encouragement about right now. Has anyone helped you in this group? Do something special for him or her. Today we honor our mentors.

SECTION THREE

A REVOLUTION OF HEALING THE HEART

Growing Deeper

CHURCH GROWTH AND deeper spirituality are passions of mine. I love to see the creative work of God in a community of people fulfilling His powerful plan. For over twenty years I have been professionally involved with traditional, mega church, and missional growth movements in America. The context of the church in which I served began in the inner city of a dying town filled with violence, drugs, and victimization. I found the church growth movements inspirational, but contemporary music, drama, purpose statements, and ideological analysis cannot touch the deepest hurts of post modern addicts and survivors of trauma.

I have great respect for the mega churches, their leadership, style, and passion. Truthfully, however, over ninety percent of the churches in America are not mega and never will be. If research data and post modern prophets are accurate, Christian culture will be moving away from the mega corporations to small informal gatherings in the next twenty years. There must be biblical, God-driven answers for the majority of denominations and local church communities not located in mega population centers. The question is: are there deeper issues of growth other than mega purpose bullet points and prophetic statements from the emergent church movement? Can a more relevant and therefore more powerful perspective unearth?

Standing with my ministry buddies, hands in pockets, we talk Detroit Piston basketball, and someone says it: "So, what's the membership of your parish up to? How big is your budget? How many staff?" We stand mute until the guy with the largest church humbly gives the number, and the rest sigh in shame. Some have termed this Parish Envy. The message is clear: big churches have greater value. But large parishes comprise a very small piece of the pie in America. Most churches range 70-90 in attendance. Church growth movements can reinforce consumerism.

You know, bigger is better. The budgets and the book sales falsely equate with deeper truth. It is possible to justify ecclesiastical existence by counting noses and nickels rather than the richer truths of Scripture. No one gives high fives to pastors in America with struggling budgets and attendance charts that bounce around like errant jump shots. But we need to. This is where treasure hides.

Sometimes when I attend church growth workshops led by world famous leaders, I feel like a hopeful but hapless high school player signing up for one mini-camp after another. I love sports. Basketball is terrific, LeBron James, Shaquille O'Neal. Awesome physics and physiques. Wanting to improve my game I sign up for "Shaquille O'Neal's slam-dunk basketball camp". I attend his seminar with my ball and ministry buddies. I position next to the Shaq eyeball to navel, mine and his respectively, staring at his size 20-something EEE shoe and the 10-foot rim. He instructs me to clear the lane with my shoulder, drop step, and slam. Easy. I clear, drop step, and clear three inches of air. Can't do it. Because I love basketball, I run, jump and slam into the wall. I sprint faster, harder, take classes in advanced leaping. Still, I can't slam dunk. The passion is right, but the physics fail.

Next, I find a world class coach-mentor named Bill Hybels. Coach Hybels is athletic, tan, chiseled. A franchise player himself he launched his mini-camp from a movie theater. Since the theater days, he built multi-million dollar church facilities coaching tens of thousands excited fans weekly. Bill coaches me to add music and drama to my slam-dunk workout. I listen to tapes, purchase the tools, attend seminars. I create a small group program with other basketball players to hold me accountable. I study the basketball psychology of Slam-dunkin' Sam, a baby boomer who grew up hating sports . . . boring, he says. Sam was always picked last and resents athletes. Now with an integrity-filled relationship I invite Sam to my workout. The contemporary music and comedic sketches execute with excellence. I am told that the key to success is gifted players and coaching. Coach Bill gives me a seven step slam dunking strategy. My uniform is pro. I look like a franchise player, but I can't touch the rim at 5'9". My shoe size not quite 23 EEE.

Next I read the "Purpose Driven Slam Dunker". Coach Rick Warren is not so lean and athletic, but I like the neat list of purpose statements and cool memory devices spelling words. He began his coaching dynasty in a tent. Since his tent meeting take off, he too built a mega corporate church campus serving tens of thousands each week. Instead of a slick franchise pro uniform I wear Hawaiian flowered shorts in the tradition of my mentor. The slam-dunking results fire me up! Sprawling campus, millions of best selling coaching manuals sold, saved lives, ministry mecca!

A new guy coaches down south, Joel Osteen. His camp is huge, like Texas. He dunks gentle and slow like his southern drawl. Coach Osteen learned to slam dunk among the rich oil fields of the Lone Star State. Joel's manual is entitled "Enjoying Your Best Game Now." His sporting events loom large; cameras scan the arena showing tens of thousands of hungry fans. Building, expanding, Coach Osteen teaches success in seven steps.

With a renewed attitude, a mini-camp manual under my arm, and a fistful of teaching cd's, I then drive back onto the rental property of our church in a violent neighborhood with broken lives. Something is wrong. I feel a sense of shame as though I just walked into the women's locker room by accident. The seminars don't cover this. The mega churches record larger Sunday attendance than the entire population of the city I serve in. Reality check. I'm no franchise player in a megatropolis. I'm a short preacher who can't jump. But I love the Lord. The exhilaration of leading other broken basketball players to the rim is the best thing on the planet. Lives change; hope emerges in impossible circumstances. That fires me up!

Can there be a perspective on church growth that fits my feet and neighborhood with a deeper spirituality for others who can't touch the rim?

The mega churches brought renewed vision to the church in America. The church growth movement as expressed in huge gatherings have value in their venue. They also fail to identify with the overwhelming majority of local communities of believers. The bigness can communicate unreal expectations. The marketing of tools, book sales, and budgets has the potential to trigger deeper addictions to success in a consumerist society. Theologian, Dr. Gilbert Bilezikian witnessed the birth of the mega church movement in the 70's. He personally mentored mega church leaders adding a biblical framework to phenomenal growth. Dr. Bilezikian, regarding one large ministry, states that the mega church "was on target originally," he says, "but there's always the temptation to seek success, as defined by the world, meaning preoccupation with numbers, with business, with facilities, and as a result there is always a danger for a church to become bureaucratic and hierarchical" (McNeil, ANS). The Shaq will encourage you and inspire you. But if you try to slam dunk, you will end up looking quite ridiculous.

Over ninety percent of churches in America are small communities of faith. There is treasure near and I believe this makes God's heart beat fast. In simpler terms I wonder if we look at "big" churches and we see "better". I think it time we examine the majority of church communities and declare, "deeper".

From our first organizational meeting to the largest service to date the inner city church grew many times over. The start was not in a theater, tent, or oil field, but in an inner-city war zone filled with crime, drugs, and heartbreak. In this environment hard core post modern people came to faith growing in loyalty and love for God. In the inner city another way to "be and do" church discovered us.

If the emergent missional church movement is your game, you have already crossed the bridge that historical growth ideology cannot score for a post modern church. My prayer is that you will uncover a treasure in these pages bringing a depth of wholeness to your heart and the hurt people you worship with. You will find no steps to success, no purpose statements, no programming tips, no size 20-something basketball shoes, and absence of rage and cynicism. But you will find First-Century sandals, Air-Galileans, leading you to a pathway of wholeness and grace.

Small Group Bible Study

Read together this great treasure passage from Matthew 6 in several translations. Try to capture different nuances. You will love this. Look for the treasure of a deep life with Jesus.

Do not store up for yourselves treasures on earth, where moth and rust destroy, and where thieves break in and steal. But store up for yourselves treasures in heaven, where moth and rust do not destroy, and where thieves do not break in and steal. For where your treasure is, there your heart will be also. The eye is the lamp of the body. If your eyes are good, your whole body will be full of light. But if your eyes are bad, your whole body will be full of darkness. If then the light within you is darkness, how great is that darkness! No one can serve two masters. Either he will hate the one and love the other, or he will be devoted to the one and despise the other. You cannot serve both God and Money. Therefore I tell you, do not worry about your life, what you will eat or drink; or about your body, what you will wear. Is not life more important than food, and the body more important than clothes? Look at the birds of the air; they do not sow or reap or store away in barns, and yet your heavenly Father feeds them. Are you not much more valuable than they? Who of you by worrying can add a single hour to his life?

And why do you worry about clothes? See how the lilies of the field grow. They do not labor or spin. Yet I tell you that not even Solomon in all his splendor was dressed like one of these. If that is how God clothes the grass of the field, which is here today and tomorrow is thrown into the fire, will he not much more clothe you, O you of little faith? So do not worry, saying, "What shall we eat?" or "What shall we drink?" or "What shall we wear?" For the pagans run after all these things, and your heavenly Father knows that you need them. But seek first His kingdom and His righteousness, and all these things will be given to you as well. Therefore do not worry about tomorrow, for tomorrow will worry about itself. Each day has enough trouble of its own.
Matthew 6:19-25 NIV

1. Make a list of all the "do nots". Jesus gets very personal about our spiritual life doesn't he? Talk about the "do nots" in this passage.

2. Can you find the one positive statement in this passage. Can you contrast it with the "do nots"? I wonder if this intends to be the great energy of our life with Jesus?

3. This positive statement connects to the heart. Can you see how deep this is? Talk about what it will mean to apply this passage in your life right now. Can you connect this statement to materialism, the economy, the pursuit of more?

4. The word pagan comes from the latin word pagani which means people who dwell outside of the city. The pagani crafted their own idolatrous religions disconnected from the mainline faith movements of the civilized world. Pagans and Christians are defined in this passage. Write out the differences. Talk about this together.

5. Can you see that worry impacts deep spirituality with Jesus? Talk about your greatest worries. Remember that anxiety launches addiction and the crazy thinking of trauma. How can you surrender your worries? How can you help each other?

Writing Your Story, Healing Your Heart

In this chapter you probably caught an attitude in my writing. I have a sense of being sold church growth programs by world famous leaders. I think growth is much more personal and less program oriented. The first century church launched without cool stuff and programs. They loved Jesus and found depth in community. In a way I write my story of disillusionment with church programs. Can you write your own story of disappointment with church organizations, denominations, and programs? Were you hurt by church folk? Can you end your story with treasure? Share your story and write about it below.

Write Your Story

Write Your Story

GOD DNA

All Scripture is God breathed. 2 Timothy 3:16 GNT

A DEEPER, RICHER facet of the spiritual life emerges under-the-radar and possesses intrinsic value. This treasure is Jesus Christ through His Spirit, listening, helping, and bringing wholeness to broken lives within small groups of Christians. The treasure cannot be buildings, pastors, bullet point growth strategies, or religion. A friend of mine sent this email to me on religious thinking.

FOUR RELIGIOUS TRUTHS

1. Muslims do not recognize Jews as God's chosen people.
2. Jews do not recognize Jesus as the Messiah.
3. Protestants do not recognize the Pope as the leader of the Christian World.
4. Evangelicals do not recognize each other at Hooters restaurant.

Historically religious and mega church strategists generate lists and steps to growth; the Spirit in biblical community creates wholeness and balance within the rhythms of his grace.

The next question is, what truths guided us in the 'hood?

God's word warns us of danger and directs us to hidden treasure.
Psalm 19:11 MSG

My child, treasure my instructions. Tune your ears to wisdom, and concentrate
on understanding. Cry out for insight and understanding. Search for them as
you would for lost money or hidden treasure. Then you will understand what
it means to fear the Lord, and you will gain knowledge of God.
Proverbs 2:1-4 NIV

Growth in the inner city happened in a healing community of believers discovering the riches of Christ's presence in the Scriptures. The Scriptures are like God-DNA possessing His holiness, love, and personality.

My dad has Parkinson's, Alzheimer's, diabetes, and an enlarged heart. He often becomes disoriented, forgets birthdays and falls down. Fortunately, decades of consuming countless half gallon containers of ice cream have calcium-fortified his stocky frame from splintering when he heel reels and falls. Though aging and ill, when I kiss him, I recall my childhood. I remember the smell of coffee-laced kisses at bedtime. The aroma still lingers in his skin, his breath, it is his DNA. He sits in a wheelchair now, I kiss his forehead, and the kiss tastes the same. Memory traces trigger boyhood images of the heroic man who carried me broken and bleeding into the ER. Like Mel Gibson in a scene from Braveheart, Dad carried my limp body in his arms shouting commands to medical staff. I see his blue painted face standing tall in plaid Bermuda shorts, hard soled wingtips, black dress socks, and a white undershirt with gravy stains. His DNA is in his kiss. I sense it now. A kiss acquires power because you share the breath of another. You receive into your soul the DNA of one you love. Scripture is the breath of God. In His word divine DNA transfers to the human heart. In His DNA the strand of his character, being, will, love, and sensitivity emerge.

Wholeness for addicts and survivors unearths through Jesus Christ healing in intimate community. The pathway is God DNA, the Scriptures. Beginning at lunch tables in cheap pizza joints, construction sites, homes, to our building in the 'hood we held on with white knuckles to applying His word in small groups. We practiced honesty, sharing lives, praying for and serving each other, and God's grace gripped us.

Our experience of Scripture and intimate healing community is not unique. I researched the toughest target groups on the planet to find out how God brings wholeness to them. Teen Challenge, a recovery ministry for addicts, focuses on a rigorous yearlong course of biblical study with intensive discipleship. Research shows almost eight out of ten people who complete the Teen Challenge program stay in recovery. They have productive lives. Eighty-seven percent go on to college. Eighty percent are employed. Seventy-six percent support themselves. Seventy-five percent continue not to use drugs. God and His word within intimate Christian community bring wholeness to addicted lives (Kenny, 1995).

Chuck Colson, former Watergate conspirator, founded Prison Fellowship. Convicted and sent to prison, Colson found Christ and began this ministry to inmates. The Academy of Criminal Justice Sciences in its Justice Quarterly reports that inmates who participate in ten or more Prison Fellowship Bible studies are sixty six percent less likely to return to prison. Some of the toughest people on the planet find wholeness and help in prison small group Bible studies (Johnson, 1997).

The Baldwin Research Institute conducted a study of Alcoholics Anonymous. Baldwin reports that AA had a ninety three percent success rate before the institutionalization of the program. When AA operated from its spiritual roots with willing participants, over nine out of ten alcoholics found wholeness and healing. Wounded-addicted people sit in a small group and discuss one of twelve Biblical principles for healing and help (Baldwin, 2004).

Addicts and survivors have found power in intimate biblical community, deep and rich. But data shows that small groups focusing on God's word now crosses into the mainstream of American spirituality. George Barna has polled the spiritual pulse of the nation for many years. His research discovered a growing movement of tens of millions of post modern Americans he calls "revolutionaries." He defines revolutionaries:

> They have no use for churches that play religious games, whether those games are worship services that drone on without the presence of God or ministry programs that bear no spiritual fruit. Revolutionaries eschew ministries that compromise or soft sell our sinful nature to expand organizational turf. They refuse to follow people in ministry leadership positions who cast a personal vision rather than God's, or who seek popularity rather than the proclamation of truth in their public statements or who are more concerned about their own legacy than that of Jesus Christ. They refuse to donate one more dollar to man made monuments that mark their own achievements and guarantee their place in history. They are unimpressed by accredited degrees and endowed chairs in Christian colleges and seminaries that produce young people incapable of defending the Bible or unwilling to devote their life to serving others. And Revolutionaries are embarrassed by language that promises Christian love and holiness but turns out to be all sizzle and no substance (Barna, p. 12).

Barna goes on to say that revolutionaries find strength and meaning in real community applying God's word. This same wholeness addicts and survivors found in the inner city. Barna cites seven passions of the revolutionary; 1) Intimate Worship with Others. Sunday morning celebration events are wonderful. I love driving to church service with my family to exalt God together. Signing a tithe check so Christ can be honored rocks! Sunday morning becomes a starting point. A deeper journey touches intimacy, belonging with a group of healing believers, enjoying the wonder of His presence. Transformational Christians pray and challenge with their example. Their words convey a deep love for God's word proclaiming its power and relevance in their lives; 2) Faith-based Conversations. We are God's treasure. He loves us, thinks about us, and pursues. People who find healing and grace naturally talk about it to others. These low-profile, high-impact conversations form the grassroots of relational evangelism. In the growth of our church this key multiplies disciples. One healing person shares the story of how God's word and grace touched them, and then another; 3) Intentional Spiritual Growth. When Christ forgives and healing happens, desire for more escalates. Believers who encounter Jesus Christ have an amazing attitude. They perceive others as God's treasure, they see intrinsic value ascribed to humanity. Forgiven people forgive. Healed people seek the same supernatural presence for others. Faith centers their actions seeking opportunities to grow deeper; 4) Servanthood. Living to serve rather than to be served-this is the purpose of Christ's ministry. Servanthood happens in healing communities. Tenderness, concern, empathy define revolutionary doctrine. Love becomes more than a feeling; it is an event of giving selflessly; 5) Resource Investment. Barna states, "The first Christians defined communal living through their sacrificial sharing of everything they had. Note that the scriptures specifically tell us that they shared everything with those in need. They used the variety of resources at their disposal-money, food, clothing, housing, relationships, influence, skills, time-for the benefit of all believers" (Barna, p. 20). This community sharing happened naturally in small groups of house churches; 6) Spiritual Friendships. Jesus developed more than twelve disciples; he created friendships, belonging, and intimacy. The early church loved to be together. Healing addiction and trauma in small groups forms deep relationships, bonds of mutual accountability, and integrity; 7) Family Faith. The early church gathered for temple and synagogue worship events. The foundation of the church, however, was the house church. Families found faith together. Adults modeled friendship, resource investment, servanthood, faith-based conversations, and intimate worship for children. Authentic transformational faith wove through the fabric of family life (Barna, pp. 18-20).

These seven passions form the foci of the early church and the deeper spirituality found within the great healing movements today. This research gives another line of evidence for the power of biblical community. In the year 2000, seventy percent of the population expressed their spirituality within the walls of the local church. Barna predicts, based on national research studies, that by the year 2025, thirty five percent of the population will experience and express their faith in small group communities of Christians instead of traditional churches, clearly a fifty percent reduction. Barna's research shows that grace-filled communities of Christians in small groups applying God's word will be the standard for most post modern believers, not only addicts and survivors. God's treasure of intimate healing community becomes the norm, not the exception (Barna, p. 39).

Two dynamics emerge for bringing wholeness to hard core post moderns. The first is God's word. The Scriptures always stand as a part of our lives as a church family. The focus of the healing work in Teen Challenge is God's word in the context of Christian community. Although AA meetings don't break out Bibles, participants experience thoroughly biblical principles. Prison Fellowship focuses on God's word with a captive audience in community.

And then the second component of the equation . . . His word in healing community. Plato theorized it. Luke experienced it. Jesus Christ, His Spirit healing in intimate groups of believers, holds the post modern church together. For a church in the inner city we didn't read books on community and implement it as a program. Programs don't work. The 'hood was too violent, the people too hurt. His word in small groups became our survival. The treasure was not our religion, not part of creedal formulae, but the means by which we had church the next week. This unearths the richness we found.

I spoke with my father recently. He slurs his words, forgets his thoughts, but I remember his kiss and the aroma of coffee. I reflect back to the embrace of strong arms, his William Wallace courage in Bermuda shorts and wingtips accessorized with black dress socks. Dad forgot my last birthday, but his DNA lives in my heart.

Small Group Bible Study

1. I like this passage of Scripture. What kind of danger has God's word kept you from? Think about your story and reflect on the power of the treasure to help you.

> *God's word warns us of danger and directs us to hidden treasure.*
> *Psalm 19:11 MSG*

2. In Proverbs 2 the writer gives us some great verbs which connect to embracing the Scriptures. List those verbs and talk about them.

3. There is a great result when we treasure Scripture. The verse ends with *Then you will understand what it means . . . .* What are the results?

> *My child, treasure my instructions. Tune your ears to wisdom, and concentrate on understanding. Cry out for insight and understanding. Search for them as you would for lost money or hidden treasure. Then you will understand what it means to fear the Lord, and you will gain knowledge of God.*
> *Proverbs 2:1-4 NIV*

Writing Your Story, Healing Your Heart

I studied for years in seminary enduring boring lectures on church history. A-G-O-N-Y. One lecture sticks with me to this day. The professor finished a series of dissertations on faith movements which embraced God's word and those which did not. Historically faith communities which honored and revered the Scriptures endured, those which did not perished. Great stuff. Tell the group about the power of God's word in your faith journey. What Scriptures have touched you, inspired you, changed you? Talk about this with your group. Below write your story of God's word changing you. How has God's word touched your marriage, your singleness, your family, your market place matters, your morality?

Write Your Story

Write Your Story

Belonging

A SIGNIFICANT BODY OF work by American authors today researches the impact of post modern influence on Christianity. Post modernism technically designates a generation of people who do not assume foundational principles. Truth for the post modern is not absolute. Truth tracks through truculent rapids of change. Post modern people need to experience a sense of belonging. The post modern seeker of Christ requires belonging before the believing takes place. He must find a niche, an acceptance, honest friendship, real relationships before she signs on the bottom line and writes a check to support ministry.

The need to belong accentuates with post modern addicts and survivors of trauma. Deep within the alcoholic feels unsettled, shamed, abandoned. He medicates this pain. The closest ally violated the survivor. She feels blame for the assault, esteem hemorrhages, she may repeat patterns of abuse volunteering violation again and again. She trusts no one. Self-loathing lingers. A loving Creator is not only a remote concept; she may even place the face of her perpetrator on God.

Let's go to Scripture and examine one of Jesus' messages of belonging.

Now the tax collectors and sinners were all gathering
around to hear Him (Jesus).
Luke 15:1 NIV

Notice that the people who loved to be near Jesus and listen were IRS agents, addicts, and the traumatized. Sounds like the 'hood. What attracts the toughest crowd on the planet? Belonging. Jesus exuded a sense that people fit into God's plan. The roughest refugee feels right about listening to God.

But the Pharisees and the teachers of the law muttered,
"This man welcomes sinners and eats with them."
Luke 15:2 NIV

Enter Perfect People Syndrome. The perfect people mutter again, critical of "those people". The IRS agents, addicts, and survivors don't appear to be in the right place. But the broken people engage in an activity that the perfect people cannot . . . listening. Think for a moment about the processes of aversion attachment and idolatry. IRS agents, addicts, and survivors cause me anxiety. They smell like cigarette smoke, and the stench of alcohol oozes from their pores. My separation and rejection ease feelings of anxiety. Neurons habituate to create a new balance. Then it happens. An imperfect person confronts me. Their brokenness causes me anxiety; I react with irritability, anger, disgust. Withdrawal. Like the perfect people in this account I deny my own sin and shame, rationalize that they do not belong, and blame someone else for welcoming them into the community of faith.

Then Jesus told them this parable.
Luke 15:3 NIV

Jesus accepted not only the IRS agents, addicts, and survivors, but also the perfect people. This shows the depth of God's character. He loves the very people who would eventually betray His son. They too belong to God. Amazing grace. As I survey my ministry, the deepest hurts and greatest brokenness have come from the hands of perfect people. The plastic smiles and pious platitudes betray shame and inner failure. Perfect people aren't. They can't be faultless, and for this they are the treasure of God's heart.

Suppose one of you has a hundred sheep and loses one of them. Does he not
leave the ninety-nine in the open country and go after the lost sheep until he
finds it? And when he finds it, he joyfully puts it on his shoulders and goes
home. Then he calls his friends and neighbors together and says, "Rejoice with
me. I have found my lost sheep!" I tell you that in the same way there will be
more rejoicing in heaven over one sinner who repents than over ninety-nine
righteous persons who do not need to repent.
Luke 15:4-7 NIV

Look at the character of God. The father embraces his missing treasure. There's more. God has joy. He calls his small group to his house and shares the delight with them. A young man in his twenties met me after a church service. He told me his life melted down when he messed up. A tough alcoholic, his biological parents coerced him to sell drugs as a six-year-old child. When the little boy failed, they rubbed his face in dog excrement as punishment. He came to faith and I baptized him in Lake Michigan. Later I married him to his sweetheart. God loves lost sheep. They belong. Vital to healing wounded hearts is not flinching when horror stories unfold. Belonging, acceptance, joy, celebration form the appropriate responses to brokenness.

Jesus paints a second picture of belonging. *"Or suppose a woman has silver coins and loses one. Does she not light a lamp, sweep the house and search carefully until she finds it? And when she finds it, she calls her friends and neighbors together and says, 'Rejoice with me; I have found my lost coin.' In the same way I tell you there is rejoicing in the presence of the angels of God over one sinner who repents." Luke 15:8-10 NIV*

I like the image of God searching carefully, meticulously seeking treasure. Again, he calls intimate friends to share in pure delight. A treasure theme. Jesus expands the community of those who find joy in belonging to the angels. All this commotion, energy, passion for IRS agents, addicts and survivors to find grace, help, and wholeness.

Jesus teaches the same message with a third picture . . . this time the most powerful.

"Jesus continued. There was a man who had two sons.
The younger one said to his father, 'Father, give me my share of the estate.'
So he divided his property between them."
Luke 15:11 NIV

Jesus uses strong Greek vocabulary here. The son asked his father for a share of reality (Scott, p. 507). The father gave him, in the Greek, bios, property (Scott, p. 130). The son wanted the real, the lasting. He desired treasure of the deepest kind. The issue is not that the father refused his demand, the son made an impossible request. He wanted to consume the treasure, rather than be transformed by it. The son's demand was not the pathway of peace, but of anesthesia. He wanted escape. This is classic addictive thinking.

"Not long after that, the younger son got together all he had, set off for a
distant country and there squandered his wealth in wild living.
After he had spent everything, there was a severe famine in that whole country,
and he began to be in need. So he went and hired himself out to a citizen of
that country who sent him to his fields to feed pigs. He longed to fill his stomach
with the pods that the pigs were eating but no one gave him anything."
Luke 15:13-14 NIV

This is the bottom of life, brokenness. Jewish piety and pork don't mix. Purity is a pillar of Judaism. Community and caring for the poor form deep systems in the Law. All seemed lost. Among the scores of addicts I counseled, not one entered recovery after a counseling session. Words don't work. The only step toward wholeness is . . . the bottom. All seems lost. An alcoholic sits with the people he or she loves and they read letters of pain and trauma. The addict faces the loss of belonging and family. At this place of brokenness denial crushes, no more rationale remains, no one else to blame. And then these words.

"When he came to his senses . . . ."
Luke 15:17 NIV

Literally the text says, "He came to himself." Defining moment. The reality he sought was not the cash, the shallow relationships, the distance; the reality he sought was belonging to the father.

"So he got up and went to his father. But while he was still a long way off,
his father saw him and was moved to compassion for him; he ran to his son,
threw his arms around him and kissed him."
Luke 15:20 NIV

The son moved from distance to nearness. The images stun. Look at the words describing what God felt and did. When the father saw the son, God was "filled with compassion." These are the strongest words possible to convey emotion. Literally the words mean his "guts churned within him" (Scott, p. 645). God ran. Near eastern estate owners were men of distinction often carried or driven by servants. The father lays down dignity. He throws his arms around a rebellious boy, and draws him close. God kisses a soiled son. Divine DNA transfers. Jesus uses a preposition – kata–with the word "kiss", painting a picture of a compassionate parent kissing his son all over his face.

The French word for kiss is *embrasser,* from which we get embrace. More than a casual peck on the cheek God engages and tenderly loves the lost son. Remarkable the emotion God possesses for an addict victimized by his impoverished pursuit of reality.

"The son said to him, 'Father, I have sinned against heaven and against you. I
am no longer worthy to be called your son.' But the father said to his servants,
'Quick, bring the best robe and put it on him. Put a ring on his finger and
sandals on his feet. Bring the fatted calf and kill it. Let's have a feast and
celebrate. For this son of mine was dead and is alive again, he was lost and is
found.' So they began to celebrate."
Luke 15:21 NIV

The son begins to deliver a pre-packaged pre-rehearsed sermon. Look at his words, "I have sinned against God and you. I am not worthy to be your son." Brokenness. Tsunami. The bottom. The clarity and honesty are rich. The son uses words which drive the emotions behind every addiction, "I am not worthy to belong." The son has never been closer to reality. The father ignores the rehearsed speech. Orders issue. Personhood restores. Community re-creates. Nearness to the father is re-instated. The son belongs.

Questions penetrate. When did the son belong to the father? Did he have a track record of perfect performance, church attendance, community service? Was he a moral pillar on an elder board? What frames the context for the belonging of the son? The son, addicted, traumatized, broken, belonged because he was the treasure of the father's heart. No lists, no performance questions. He belonged.

Let's survey the Old and New Testaments for a satellite view of belonging.

The theology starts in Genesis 2:18. When God created man . . . He said, *"It is not good for man to be alone (NIV)"* So he created a woman who, along with man, would complete the image of God Himself. Man and woman, each made in God's image, reflect divine personality and character. And together man and woman would not be alone . . . they enjoyed relationship with God and each other. Belonging.

God reminds Israel of His deliverance when he rescued them from slavery in Egypt and now He expresses his commitment to them as he gives them a new identity.

> *As Moses went up to meet God, he called down to him from the mountain:*
> *"Speak to the House of Jacob, tell the People of Israel: 'You have seen what I*
> *did to Egypt and how I carried you on eagles' wings and brought you to me.*
> *If you will listen obediently to what I say and keep my covenant, out of all*
> *peoples you'll be my special treasure. The whole Earth is mine to choose from,*
> *but you're special: a kingdom of priests, a holy nation."*
> *Exodus 19:3-6 NIV*

The treasure of belonging is not only for the people of Israel, but anyone who discovered its value.

> *Make sure no outsider who now follows God ever has occasion to say, "God put*
> *me in second-class. I don't really belong." And make sure no physically mutilated*
> *person is ever made to think, "I'm damaged goods. I don't really belong."*
> *Isaiah 56:3 MSG*

1 Peter 2:9-10 NIV contrasts those who belong to God and those who do not, and it sounds similar to what God told His people in the book of Exodus:

> *But you are not like that, for you are a chosen people. You are a kingdom of*
> *priests, God's holy nation, His very own possession. This is so you can show*
> *others the goodness of God, for He called you out of the darkness into His*

wonderful light. "Once you were not a people; now you are the people of God.
Once you received none of God's mercy; now you have received His mercy."

God singled out, chose, and declared His people special, a treasure.

Let's look at the power of belonging. God gave us our identity of belonging in community.

Therefore you are no longer outsiders (exiles, migrants, and aliens, excluded
from the rights of citizens), but you now share citizenship with the saints
(God's own people, consecrated and set apart for Himself); and you belong to
God's [own] household.
Ephesians 2:19 Amplified Bible

The word household forms a powerful term in the New Testament. In our post modern context the word household means those who live in our home. In the first century the word household consisted not only of blood relatives and those who married into the family, but also included friends, business associates, clients, employees. In other words, the household included everyone who was valuable to it. The household was a vital social community. And anyone adopted had full privileges of the blood relatives. This place expressed belonging to others through love and commitment. When the inspired writers call us "members of God's household", they tell us we have a new identity – we belong to Him and to each other. We have value to God (John Lillis, Lecture on Spiritual Formation). God's household is His treasure. He designed it to be a true family, with mutual commitment, where no one lives in isolation.

Jim Kallam in his book *Risking Church* talks about the importance of intimate community being safe, so that people have freedom to be real, to be themselves. He cites four factors necessary for belonging to exist: 1) Safety through care and nurture.

"Let's see how inventive we can be in encouraging love and helping out."
Hebrews 10:24 MSG

"And let us consider and give attentive,
continuous care to watching over one another."
Hebrews 10:24 Amplified

Care and nurture run deep. They strike the core of parent child relationships and intimate biblical community. More than lip service, they are poignant commitments to love and cherish one another.

The first Sunday after my return from a two-week vacation I rose early to pray and prepare for our worship service. I looked out the window and noticed a woman across the street sitting on a doorstep in her pajamas. Strange, but I serve in the 'hood so this kind of thing doesn't shock me. After the Terrace Street Streaker, this is pretty tame. A knock at the door. The pajama-clad woman collapsed in front of me. Though a neighbor of mine, I didn't recognize her because she had been beaten, bitten, and battered over twenty five times by her crack-head husband. Face swollen and hair soaked in her own blood she lay weeping. Early in the morning her spouse forcefully entered the home, demanded money for drugs, then assaulted her. She jumped out the second floor window to survive. He fled. She began knocking on doors. No one opened their home or heart to her. She dressed inappropriately and looked like she had been in a cage fight. She had been.

As she lay on my kitchen floor waiting for the emergency medical team, hair matted and stained red in her own blood, I could not help but think of her wedding. Dressed in beautiful clothes, hair done, nails perfect, her husband vowing to have and hold, for better for worse, in sickness and health, being faithful . . . 'til death separates. I felt crushed. Wasn't there a promise to belong, to accept, to give one's life for the sake of the other? Belonging accepts, opens doors to broken people. Belonging creates safety in adversity.

2) Vision—We believe in what you can become. *"Him we preach and proclaim, warning and admonishing everyone and instructing everyone in all wisdom (comprehensive insight into the ways and purposes of God), that we may present every person mature (full-grown, fully initiated, complete, and perfect) in Christ." Colossians 1:28 AMP.* 3) Wisdom—We will challenge each other toward deeper growth.

". . . asking God, the glorious Father of our Lord Jesus Christ, to give you spiritual wisdom and understanding, so that you might grow in your knowledge of God." Ephesians 1:17 NLT. 4) Power. This power uncovers within intimate biblical community (Kallum, pp. 35-66). *I pray that from His glorious, unlimited resources he will give you mighty inner strength through His Holy Spirit. Ephesians 3:16 NLT.*

The theology of belonging did not enter our lives because of the post modern era. Belonging weaves throughout the tapestry of God's character and His word.

"All the tax collectors, hardened sinners were really getting close to hear Him" Luke 15:1 (Greek New Testament). They drew near, very near in the original text because they belonged. They sensed it. Addicts and survivors look for acceptance in your eyes; they seek belonging in your tone of voice. I have a deep sense of honor when a victim of serial rape with multiple personalities tells me his story. I do not flinch, wrinkle my forehead, or sigh. I grieve with him, and extend the embrace of grace that gripped me. The drunks, the traumatized, saw the heart of the father in Jesus. His eyes invited, his arms accepted, His words woven with love and tenderness. They drew real close . . . to the treasure of belonging.

Let me challenge you for growth and spiritual depth in your church and community. Pray that God will give you obnoxious broken people so you can give them the gift of belonging. Grow one pajama clad heart at a time. You become a missional faith community in the market place, your school. Invite them to fit in with you. Pick the calls girls, the charlatans, and IRS assessors. A treasure unearths when we extend arms to the beaten, bitten, and bleeding. The broken people in our lives open the door of our heart to God and we belong.

Small Group Bible Study

Our work together results in maturity. Look at this passage.

"Him we preach and proclaim, warning and admonishing everyone and instructing everyone in all wisdom (comprehensive insight into the ways and purposes of God), that we may present every person mature (full-grown, fully initiated, complete, and perfect) in Christ." Colossians 1:28 AMP. As you study God's word and blend your story with his, you will see transformation take place.

1. Look at these passages on maturity. *". . . asking God, the glorious Father of our Lord Jesus Christ, to give you spiritual wisdom and understanding, so that you might grow in your knowledge of God." Ephesians 1:17 NLT.* What facets of maturity do you see in this passage? I like how he starts with . . . asking God for maturity. What other facets do you see?

2. *I pray that from His glorious, unlimited resources he will give you mighty inner strength through His Holy Spirit. Ephesians 3:16 NLT.* In this passage Paul speaks of inner strength as an aspect of maturity. The Holy Spirit gives strength and power. Can you have a conversation about God's power in your life?

3. As we create a culture of belonging, encouragement forms a large part of the process. Can you reflect on the Scriptures below and discuss how you can encourage your community. Be careful, this is infectious!

"Let's see how inventive we can be in encouraging love and helping out."
Hebrews 10:24 MSG

"And let us consider and give attentive,
continuous care to watching over one another."
Hebrews 10:24 Amplified

Writing Your Story, Healing Your Heart

Make a time line of the major events of your life. Look back at your story and put the highlights and lowlights on a time line. Share it with your group. You will need more paper than I can provide below. Use the space to outline your life. Then transfer to another larger sheet. As you record each event, can you see the presence of God at each step? Galilean footprints?

REAL Community

I RESIST LISTS and bullet point strategies for experiencing a richer spirituality of the heart. I do like memory devices. Here I give homage to my basketball coach with the Hawaiian flowered shorts, Rick Warren. He loves memory devices. Let's look at four facets of biblical community we encountered in the 'hood. I use the word "real" in contrast to virtual. Have you seen life-sized video games? Strap on virtual goggles and you live a fantasy in three dimension. It seems authentic, but it's bogus-virtual . . . not real. The nature of belonging cannot tolerate imitation.

The "R" in real stands for right through Christ. The rightness of the spiritual journey comes through Him, "*. . . filled with the fruit of righteousness that comes through Jesus Christ" Philippians 1:11 NIV.* The life change in the 'hood did not happen because of a state-of-the-art facility with contemporary music and strategic planning. Transformation happens because of the payment for our sin, forgiveness and belonging through Jesus Christ on the cross, and His resurrection from death. Think about driving into the scariest, messiest neighborhood on the planet every day. Houses decaying, crime, trauma, drugs. Paint peels from Barney purple walls. The inner city forced us to seek the deeper, the richer. We could not rely on a beautiful facility or mini camps to reach people only the message of Jesus Christ. Healing and help did not come through mega-church strategies or religion. In our community of faith bikers, Baptists, ex-strippers, Seventh Day Adventists, drunks, corporate execs, professionals, millionaires, multiple personalities, Methodists, welfare recipients, Catholics, Charismatics, crack heads, Lutherans, Reformed, former atheists, and I imagine a few Hittites, Moabites, and Cellulites worship together. This is a diverse group with deep opinions. We make it together because our reason for being is Christ.

I have a certain twisted delight in my small group when a recovering adult child of fundamentalism sits next to a dissociative identity disorder friend with a lifetime of affairs, addiction, and crime. Great fun. At times while I preach, I multi-task in my brain. While speaking, I wonder how in the world the Baptists and the Charismatics can worship together in the same room. Joy can only describe the feeling of a Catholic and a Lutheran serving together to feed the poor. A tough converted atheist called me once to say that "we were doing a XXXX of a job" serving Christ. One of our converts approached me at our baptism celebration. In front of a fundamentalist-holiness board member, the new Christian declares in decibels all can hear, "Hey pastor Glen, great day! I am proof that poop floats!" (Not the actual noun he used.) The diversity, the beauty of Christian community happens because our rightness enters through Christ.

The "E" stands for empowered by God's Spirit in community. Sunday services in a theater chair or pew do not equal intimate community. In the Old Testament the Father, Son, and Spirit–Trinitarian community–create the cosmos. In Exodus God's Spirit leads a community with fire and cloud. In Acts 2 the Holy Spirit came to a group of believers. This event at Pentecost launched the first century into transformation through small house churches. Powerful.

In terms of our idolatry, addictions, and trauma, we are healing, not healed. We need the continual empowerment and grace of God's Spirit in intimate groups of Christians. The healing and not yet healed concept is called permanence (May, pp. 89-90). Idolatry, addiction and attachment form a type of spiritual learning. This teaching-learning process happens at the cellular level. Chemical changes between neurons alter cellular makeup. Multiple systems engage. The teaching-learning becomes cemented. The brain never forgets the process of restoring balance. Have you ever heard someone say that you never really forget how to ride a bike? "Don't be anxious, it'll all come back once you get on." The permanence of idolatry, attachment and addiction poise to return with seemingly insignificant encouragement. The brain learns to do idolatry and addiction and powerfully recalls the processes that soothe stress. Old patterns of neurological responses can and will return with the smallest sensation of smell, taste, and sight. This means that we must be vigilant about our idols and addictions, continuing the journey of healing together (May, pp. 89-90).

The rightness of Christ, the transformation, the healing and belonging cause the draw of idolatry and addiction to diminish. Behavior becomes more Christ-like. But neurons do not completely forget. This is the reason Luke used the word koinonia. Its roots in classic Greek point toward the God principle holding the church together, intimate healing community. I am always in a deep small group or planning the next one.

In my group I choose to be honest about my brokenness. I talk about it. People listen. They pray and hold me accountable. This is a powerful system for healing. As I drive to my small group, I inventory my life. Who am I today? What drives my behavior? Did I kick the dog or scream at the kids? Does my wife like me? Lori must love me . . . like is optional. I also have a mentor. We meet regularly talking about the goodness of God, we pray for each other. We know the brokenness. There is no lying . . . no virtual relationship. In these intimate relationships based on His word, God's Spirit moves, guides, and heals. All of this creates a rich dependence on the living God.

There are two classic approaches for the healing of addictions: sin redemption and creation theologies. Sin redemption theology begins with clear statements of the sinfulness of humanity. Broken from within at birth, the redemptive work of Jesus Christ answers this impasse. His atonement pays the penalty for our sinfulness. The tone sounds pessimistic. Christ's redeeming work requires a personal choice. Sin redemption presses for spontaneous decision and transformation. People say that they recall the day, the instant in which they gave their life to Christ. Instant change takes place. I have heard drug users claim immediate deliverance from their lifestyle. The focus centers on the immediacy of forgiveness and healing for the individual.

Creation theology moves the entire created order to wholeness in process. This system does not deny human sinfulness, but the approach differs. The entry point is God's grace over time. God forms man as a new creature in process. Creation theology lacks the urgency of sin redemption theology. God seems more in control of the process of redemption. Although decisions are important, man appeals to God's choice to save and heal. The tone is optimism. The individual becomes part a great scheme of salvation redeeming the cosmos.

Sin redemption and creation theology can be harmonized. The addict, victim and perfect person are broken within. Forgiveness is imperative . . . now. The individual must act by surrendering, doing inventory, and making amends or healing cannot take place. But recovery also takes time. Relapse becomes a part of the journey. God has patience as he recreates broken neurology and reforms social systems to deepen healing.

Sin redemption and creation theology are two vital theological components on the continuum of healing the hurt of our heart. Sin redemption views the addict looking up from the bottom of his brokenness to a gracious God. This system reflects urgency to cease self destruction. A choice must be made to heal, to do moral inventory, to make amends. On the other hand the trauma and re-educating of neurons require time to heal in community. In recovery circles the term "time takes time" is common. God creates a new person through the successes and relapses of recovery. Creation theology views a loving father bringing His beloved to wholeness through process. God strategically uses time to bring peace and wholeness to broken neurology. He uses grace filled community recreating systems around the addict and victim to prevent relapse.

The "A" stands for acceptance unconditional. Admit everyone. I enjoy telling people publicly, if this church will take me, they will take anyone. Jesus loved the hookers and happy perfect people who weren't. Accept all.

Accept one another, then, just as Christ accepted you,
in order to bring praise to God.
Romans 15:7NIV

A young woman came to faith. She began to read the Bible. After a morning church service, she approached me and asked, "Pastor Glen, what does the Bible mean when it says that the Lord is a light to the genitals?" I have never passed a kidney stone, or had an aneurysm, but this came close. The Lord is a light to the genitals? First, I worked very hard not to contort my face. Lori says I do this when I am anxious. Then I scanned my memory bank for answers. Where in the Bible does it say that the Lord is a light to the . . . you know? Then it hit me. Gentiles. Gentiles, not genitals. The Lord is a light to the gentiles, non-Jewish peoples. This poor girl misread the word non-Jewish peoples and instead substituted a word reflecting her brokenness. A victim of serial rape by her father she interpreted Scripture through her pain. The young woman had a soiled past, three children by three different fathers. Broken lives finding grace. Another young woman had an abortion. She confessed. She was broken. In time we dedicated her other children to God. She felt her shame so deep and pervasive; I did not lecture her about killing the unborn child. I led her to the cross, to forgiveness, to the tenderness of God. Your part and mine is not to flinch, contort, or throw up. Accept without condition.

I brought a series of messages on feeding the poor and caring for hurting people in the inner city. We planned to launch a food bank with medical clinics for inner city families. As I closed the message, I asked the room to stand with me for prayer. When I said the "amen", I looked up to see an enormous man in front of me. He had considerable size, 6'5" or so, wearing a full size gray overcoat. The giant man with super-sized coat also positioned himself uncomfortably close to my face. Then he began to sing. With eyes closed, the copiously covered man in gray sang a beautiful southern-gospel song about Jesus caring for the poor. It was gorgeous really. Then he crooned another. There I stood with my Bible-belt Pavarotti in front of a room full of post modern addicts, survivors, and perfect people. He sang a third song. I grew anxious for a couple reasons. How do we get out of here? This is the inner city. What if his overcoat overlays nothing but his birthday suit? So, while he sang, I motioned for our artists to come forward. They assembled behind their instruments and when my inner city soloist took a breath I said, quite passionately,

"Let's all join together and sing our last congregational." We sang and I quickly dismissed the congregation.

After the service, I spoke with our singer. His name was Len. He walked by our building that cold day and felt compelled to come in. Len recounted his history of commitment to thirteen different mental institutions. His diagnoses ranged from schizophrenia to pyromania. On the Sunday we talked about feeding the poor and caring for our inner-city community, Len walked through the double doors. People said it seemed choreographed and scripted. I believe it was. Len would not be welcome to sing in many places. He had a shady past, a criminal record. Len was also acceptable. The glass double doors opened for him because they were cleansed by blood. A gentle carpenter skilled in driving nails turned the hammer on Himself. A tender savior through tears attached the sin and shame of Len's insanity to the cross. Christ felt the impact of Len's past, every meltdown, disappointment, and relapse. This made our urban soloist acceptable because of the shedding of blood. Clothed in a gray overcoat of grace and love Len sang a song about the treasure of his heart. I think we ought to have left the blood on the aluminum doorframe of our Barney purple building. What a powerful message . . . all are welcome and acceptable, because of the sacrifice of Christ. Follow and trust Him; His rightness covers and you belong to Him.

The "L" stands for loyalty without compromise. All of this unconditional acceptance stuff requires a bit of framework. The treasure is a relationship. By definition a relationship of love requires loyalty or relationship doesn't exist.

One of our new converts came from Chicago. A survivor of trauma, her transformation was dramatic. The converted Chicagoan learned to drive on a freeway system of twisted steel with angry motorists who at times vent with gunfire. Though our town small, at rush hour the main arteries congested. As she drove to work, a blue mini van cut her off. The woman believed, found grace and healing for her life, but old messages erupted, permanence. She became incensed and planned to give this errant motorist the bird. You know, half a peace sign, the Hawaiian good luck symbol. This is what one does when living in the fast lane and anger emerges. Vent, shoot back. The Chicagoan passed the blue mini van, slowed down, and adjusted the rear view mirror so she could get a good look when the torrid message delivered. As she fixed the mirror for the best view and delivered the bird to her victim, chagrin came across the Chicagoan when she saw me waving back at her. She gave half a peace sign to her pastor.

Loyalty to God under pressure. Where do your emotions default when under fire at freeway speeds? A pattern of loyalty in the life of Jesus Christ intrigues me. Judas plots to arrest and assassinate Jesus. We dedicate busloads of babies in our church. They have grand names like John, Paul, Mark, Matthew, Sarah, Hope, Grace, but not one named Judas. Never. Synonyms of betray are give up, hand over, inform on, let down, deceive, to be disloyal to. Judas. He was all of these and more. Jesus' response to Judas causes me anxiety. Jesus is kind, compassionate, and tender with His traitor. Judas kisses and Jesus kindly returns the gesture. Jesus transfers divine DNA to a traitor's cheek. In the scene previous, Jesus, with clean hands and a pure heart, washed the feet of His betrayer. Loyalty.

Depth uncovers here. The deepest wounds come from betrayal. The greatest act of love and belonging is loyalty.

Jesus said it, *"Love your enemies, pray for those who persecute you" Matthew 5:44 NIV.* Loyalty when others take license.

A young woman complained to me about her ex-felon husband's addiction. She found a rolled up paper dollar in his pocket. He used the bill like a straw to snort coke. She asked me to confront him so he would enter recovery. I confronted. He promised. The addiction continued. He struck back. The addict claimed that I purchased illegal drugs in our inner city neighborhood and then planted them in his home. Having purchased the narcotics, I then allegedly called the police to have him arrested. He told folks in the church about this. People listened. One attendee said to me, "Pastor Glen, why don't you confess that you planted drugs . . . we will forgive you." A drive-by shooting on integrity. Betrayal, doubt, abandonment. These are the deepest wounds of life. I thought about striking back, hiring a lawyer, hitting him hard. Then the words of Jesus Christ. Love your enemies, pray . . . . Loyalty to God when others aren't.

For an entire year our elders confronted the coke addict and he promised to deliver proof. For twelve months I was doubted and questioned. You know, the look of "How could you?" I began to pray for him. That is not easy. One afternoon I gassed up the blue mini van and met the betrayer in the station. He waited for his change. The attendant moved like molasses in Michigan winter to retrieve his money from the cash register. The betrayer's extended hand quaked. I walked to him, embraced, and said, "I have been praying for you." Not long afterward he tied a rope to the rafters in his garage, stepped off a chair, and hung himself. Be loyal in loving enemies.

Jesus is carjacked with a kiss. He kisses back. Divine character, love, and concern transfer to a disloyal disciple. An illegal court hauls Jesus in for vigilante justice and he gives silence for accusation. Loyalty to God in the most brutal circumstances.

We have communion once a month on Sunday evenings. Lovely. This event of covenant renewal, remembering, is one of my favorites. I received a call that one of our attendees lay recovering in the hospital. I thought it would be great to serve her communion after our evening service. I took with me a compact communion kit covered in purple crushed velvet. That night I used my son's car, a blue 1976 Datsun 280Z. The Z car rides low, feels like a go-cart around corners, and gets looks. Sorry, Lori, it is not about me, it's the wheels. I served my friend communion and drove home through the 'hood when I stopped at a corner to turn right. I felt great. Worship, communion, a rewarding hospital visit, doesn't get better than this.

Stopping at a traffic signal I waited for the steady traffic to clear. On my left stood Jim and Dees Grocery Mart and liquor store. I throttled the Z car feeling quite young and uncharacteristically cool. Then I heard a voice, "Hey hon, how about a date?" I revved. Again the voice and proposition. This time more direct. "Hey, wanna date?" I glanced to my left and saw the prostitute walking toward me. Thin with long, straight black hair, she wore a full-length coat with fur lapels. Target acquired and locked on, she wanted a date, the paying kind. Anxiety reaction. I felt flushed and embarrassed. Trapped by traffic she stealthed closer. Then I said it. Sometimes my brain disconnects from my mouth. I responded to the proposition with, "How yoooou doin'?" What am I thinking? Apparently I wasn't. Let's blame it on anxiety. Traffic cleared, I gunned it and went home.

Picture this. A call girl on the left and a communion kit on the right. What would it take to throw away treasure for a moment of pleasure? Who would know? It doesn't mean anything. Pleasure for treasure? Loyalty or disloyalty?

We talk much about grace and acceptance. Loyalty to God without compromise balances the equation. In the early part of the twentieth century Christians rejected alcoholics. You know, they are rigid, whiny, difficult, and self-absorbed (the drunks), not the kind of perfect people you want in your church pew. As a result, the 12 steps of Alcoholics Anonymous does not use the name Jesus Christ as higher power. Too bad. The church missed it by not accepting alcoholics. It has been our experience that a church community can grow with the toughest people on the planet in a violent environment without compromising the character of God. Call girl or communion? The answer is grace-filled loyalty to God. Open arms with a heart like Jesus. Grace with deep loyalty to God.

In this post modern millennium will we accept without condition and still be loyal to God without compromise? Possible? Imperative. Jesus did. The hookers, the addicts, the survivors, they were His treasure. Jesus remained loyal to God surrounded by drunks, trauma, perfect people, and in the clinch of betrayal. Loyalty to God with no compromise, accepting without condition. Watch conservatives criticize; listen to liberals condone. See the post modern serve up cynicism and rage for traditional leadership who cannot interpret missional language. Division. Pain. Another way unearths. Jesus is our treasure. We are His. All belong to Him. The journey moves forward with open hands; one accepts and the other holds tightly the holiness of God in Jesus Christ. Jesus says a deeper way avails. It is hidden—worth everything. When I cannot reach out, and I don't hold on, I look in my hands and they are full; not of treasure, but idols, ego-centric attachments fashioned in my image.

Real community. Our rightness is not about our perfection, but Christ's. A decision opens the door for wholeness to take place. Empowerment flows from His Spirit moving in small groups of Christians who love His word. All may enter without condition. You have time. God heals in process. Choose patience. Don't flip your pastor the bird. The community standard? The deepest loyalty to God possible.

Small Group Bible Study

Accept one another, then, just as Christ accepted you,
in order to bring praise to God.
Romans 15:7NIV

1. Read the passage above in several translations. Discuss how we accept one another. We accept as we have been accepted. All this brings what to God? In Luke 15.1 The Scriptures say that all the sinners came to Jesus. The Greek word means, they drew near. Why do hard core people come to Christ? Can you talk about acceptance in your group, do you ever think we become a Christian club or clique?

"Love your enemies, pray for those who persecute you" Matthew 5:44 NIV

2. Loyalty is a deep word. Plastic piety becomes no match for loyalty when you feel betrayed. Can you talk about betrayal in your life? Who did it? Were you able to remain faithful to Jesus while betrayed?

Gracie's Story

Much of the last decade blurs. It is only over the last year that God has sanitized my mind, allowing me to reflect on where I have been. Some of this story is supplemented by my husband, Jim, who fortunately/unfortunately has been there for the "ride." The individual events and stories seem infinite and perhaps unnecessary for my message here.

I cannot pinpoint when the evil destruction of addiction overwhelmed me, but honestly, I admit that I was overwhelmed within a very short time. I have learned no matter what the temptation, addiction is the same; cunning; baffling; all progressive and all consuming; a monster of enormous potency.

The eating disorder, identified as "ED" commenced his relationship with me at the age of 15. ED has been my "companion" for about 14 years. He has always tried to masquerade himself as my closet friend, in spite of his travels with me from recovery center to recovery center, hospital to hospital, and his nearly killing me on multiple occasions. During my college years, already in a weakened and vulnerable state, ED and ETOH (the acronym for Ethyl Alcohol) began their war over me to decide which of them was going to take my life and soul. You see, both of these addictions emanate from the same place of anxious fear.

My 4th trip to a recovery center was preceded by a 10 day hospital stay, in intensive care due to kidney failure. My mother flew from Michigan personally transporting me and my 72 pound skeleton to rehab for dual diagnosis recovery. My intended 90 day stay was cut short and I immediately found myself in a different rehabilitation center in Ohio. 35 days later I moved back home. Simply, I was still devoid of spirit and not yet ready. ED and ETOH immediately began their tug of war over me. It was a draw for them and a loss for me.

Over the next 3 ½ years my self-inflicted abuse resulted in an additional 130 days in rehabilitation hospitals, approximately 30 ambulance transports, and an estimated 70 days in various other hospitals. These include 3 events of respiratory arrest, tracheal intubations, ventilators, the intravenous entry into my carotid and femoral arteries("main-lining"), coma, acid-like potassium irrigations to stabilize my heart, and the involuntarily application of physical restraints. All of these procedures were medically necessary, and all of which comprise only a sliver of the enormous trauma experienced by my family and me. The highest blood-alcohol-level .64, 8 times the legal limit, was recorded at the hospital with lethal potassium levels of .9. The medical community treating me was stunned that I exited the hospital alive, let alone not brain dead, or blind.

My husband Jim, while consumed with the travel, the pressure, and the hours of running a large national corporation, soon found himself overwrought at all ends, sitting 24 hour bedside vigils, holding my hand and encouraging me to breathe when the hospital's ventilator alert would scream upon my failure to do so. He was unfairly interrogated by law enforcement authorities on several occasions with suspicions of abusing me, all due to my elaborate bruising and open wounds, caused by my drunken falls onto the tile floors in our home.

On one Saturday morning, out of control, and unable to bear the pain of my circumstances, I took one last dive into my grave hoping it would end. I performed the disappearing act from home and commenced my binge. After being discovered unconscious in a commercial shopping center, I was again rushed to the hospital via ambulance. The local hospital personnel were growing tired of their frequent experience with me, and I was discharged later that night, still inebriated. I received a cab ride back to the very same commercial area, and immediately set out drinking with a fury. Days later I woke up in the hospital. After migrating from life support to "attendant care," I found my personal attendant temporarily absent. That opening was all I needed. I tore out my life sustaining IV's, removed my monitors, and fled the hospital, where law enforcement was waiting for my release.

You see, my attorney husband was out of time, out of talk, and after 6 years of this nonsense, out of resources. He had already commenced his legal strategy to use the justice system, in order to save my life and my soul. My entry into the justice system began after being found passed out drunk in a parked car, on a public street. Because of the level of my intoxication, a condition of my DUI sentencing imposed that I could consume no alcohol. I was later informed that Jim had educated the local police department as to the legal effect of the Court's DUI probation order; and, that he pleaded for and demanded their assistance to remove me from any environment where I could obtain alcohol. I now know that the anticipated results of his plan were coming to fruition. The legal hook that enabled law enforcement was that I continued to drink.

Approximately one month later, I was rushed back to the hospital in respiratory arrest, this time monitored by law enforcement until conscious, and then taken directly to jail for violating my DUI probation – not to consume alcohol, anytime, anywhere.

I went through detox incarcerated, without medical assistance, but loaded with benzodiazepines to keep me from dying of delirium tremors. God is in control and he works in mysterious ways. Despite the horror and the terror of my liberty being taken from me, I strangely felt relief being behind bars, because being a slave to alcohol was not possible in jail. Physical withdrawal in jail was rough. I experienced 2 grand-mal seizures, but incredibly, during each seizure a "fellow inmate" was standing there to catch me when my neurological system short-circuited and I free-fell to the ground.

Not knowing my fate and with no end in sight to my confinement, I was chained and shackled like the worst of criminals, and forced to attend court appearance after court appearance in my inmate jumpsuit. I soon learned that my husband was attending every Court hearing, not to provide legal representation, and certainly not to bail me out, but rather, to monitor the proceedings and to insure that the Court would force me into the care I needed, with resulting consequences if I failed to comply. During the 105 days of incarceration I spent in the jail, I began to look at myself in the mirror of truth, no longer wanting to live Satan's lie. While incarcerated, my great grandfather passed from this earth and I was not there; my baby sister was married and I was supposed to be her maid of honor, but I was not there; my family needed me and I was not there. Broken, I became determined to no longer allow my addictions to take my joy from me, or to rob me of precious memories.

I endured the humiliation from the public rebuking of a stern judge who informed my husband in written correspondence between them, that she was "determined to save my life, or at least prolong for as long as she could." Through the grace of God, I was given the last chance to grasp recovery, or the choice of facing harsh legal, life, and spiritual consequences. The judge gave me the opportunity to complete a court ordered, six-month residential recovery, substance abuse program. The tough, but nurturing environment gave unborn children the opportunity to survive and women like me, tools to live and to be strong.

When I walked through the door of my latest rehab little did I know that every night I would be lulled to sleep by the sound of gun shots. I committed myself to recovery. I was shortly assigned the hardest duty in the house, "Kitchen Coordinator." Oh the irony, humor, and the providence with how God can work– placing an anorexic in charge of feeding, meal planning, shopping, and cooking 3 meals per day, for 16 women in recovery, often irritable. My scheduled 2 week assignment evolved into Kitchen Coordinator for nearly my entire stay, along with assignments of "Council," responsible for enforcing the house' rules and policies. My trust; integrity; self-esteem; love for myself; and, spirituality began restoration during these difficult times. I had the wonderful experience of being a doula for one of the pregnant women in the house. I felt blessed to walk through the experience with her. She had major obstacles, no trust, and no one to lean on in her time of need. The experience resulted in the amazing birth of a healthy baby girl, now adopted by a loving family.

My mandatory 6 month stay turned into 8 months. It must have been the 5:00 a.m. wakeups, the all day chores, and the cooking that lured me to request another 2 months (lol). Sober, the discipline was reforming me.

I soaked up the experiences relayed to me and the wisdom of the woman who coordinates the program, who fortunately became my counselor. She is a tiny former addict, 21 years sober, whose young son died due to complications from his drug abuse; a son she gave birth to at age 13. She is an intensely spiritual and faithful woman that lives her recovery and gives so much in her assistance to others with spiritual and life obstacles. She taught me much, now eternally tattooed in my brain: "It is only the dying who are able to hear the message;" "Where much is given, much will be required;" "Plan for the harvest and pick up your hoe;" and, she kept insisting to everyone – "Don't leave before the miracle happens." I finally realized that instead of saying "Why me?" I needed to add a word and say "Why NOT me?"

I graduated from rehab and I return once per week to visit and to exhibit to others old and new to addiction, that recovery can happen, and it will happen, if you intently seek it from the right source. For me that is God! My hope is to start an alumni group to foster hope in others.

I am reminded of my devout mother repeating to me over the course of my addiction: "Gracie, stop telling God how big your storms are and start telling your storms how BIG your God is!"

I have earnestly prayed that more would be revealed to me. It has, and continues to be revealed. God is never finished blessing. I had not been feeling well, so I visited my physician who ordered some tests, revealing that we were 6 weeks pregnant. Staggering! The eating disorder had such an impact on my body, and had so deceived my mind that I did not believe motherhood was possible for me. I recently celebrated one of year sobriety from the eating disorder and alcohol, in addition to 10 weeks of pregnancy! In my 24th week of pregnancy and 15 months of sobriety, all lab, radiological, and physical signs reveal that growing within me is a maturing, normal, and healthy baby boy, with a strong heart. Praise God!

I have gained so much strength through God. When I reflect on the past 14 years, the damage caused to everything around me, and while contemplating how many times I should have died, I know that God has given me His amazing grace.

I am grateful to all of my beloved friends, and to my family, extended and immediate. I was challenged by our "distance," but you never gave up me, and I know that you never quit praying that the power of God would persevere in righting my life and soul. I am so grateful for the love and healing. Gracie

Writing Your Story, Healing Your Heart

Finish your time line, this is a lot of work, yes? Make sure you time line the betrayals in your life. Share with your group, this will take a couple of weeks. Talk about it with your small group. Do you see God working in the broken places of your life?

The Treasure of My Heart . . . The Bride

How sweet is your love, my treasure, my bride! How much better it is than wine . . . You are like a private garden my treasure, my bride! You are like a spring that no one else can drink from, a fountain of my own.
Song of Solomon 4:10-12 NLT

PLEASE HONOR ME by finishing this work with a discussion about the treasure of my heart . . . my wife. Lori's loyalty and love for God are two of many reasons our inner-city church launched. She possesses an ocean of character and commitment. Her heart tenderness draws me. How sweet is your love my treasure, my bride!

The memories of Lori giving birth to our children still bring me to tears. Lori lay in the birthing room pregnant with Daniel, the guy with the Z car. Lori had particularly difficult deliveries, something about a scooped uterus. But there I stood, the supportive husband. Do you remember your first delivery? For our first child we arrived hours early and had to be sent home anxious and inexperienced. By the second child I believed myself an expert on birthing children. Remember the Lamaze classes and dress rehearsals for your first baby? Then for the second child you forget it. Breathing doesn't help the excruciating pain anyway and you request morphine at admission. Recall the delight of holding, rocking, and feeding the firstborn? Diapers change systematically, dropped pacifiers sterilize before re-entry, and you call the baby sitter multiple times when gone? By the second child diapers convert when they sag around chubby knees, contaminated pacifiers are squirted with a bottle of chocolate milk, wiped on a shirt tail and popped back in. By the second child, when you go on a date you instruct the baby sitter to call only if she sees blood. An old hat, I considered myself an expert on delivery . . . until aversion attachment.

Lori, in the throes of labor, contracted, grimaced, dilated, and then . . . blood. Her IV malfunctioned and plasma pooled on the floor. Low velocity spatter. I do not do blood. Nausea. Anxiety reaction. I hate throwing up. Aversion attachment. The room began to spin. I got hot. Sweat seeped. I thought to myself, "Self, I can pass out on the floor like an idiot or lie down on the delivery table next to Lori and look like an idiot." So, being the man I am, I lay down on the delivery table next to my writhing wife seconds from delivery. I realized something about Lamaze classes. Those breathing exercises may not help the mom, but they really do come in handy when you pass out next to your pregnant wife. As I lay in a quasi-comatose state, I heard an angelic voice; Lori prayed for me! Between gut wrenching contractions, Lori prayed for her knight in tarnished armor with a calm tender tone, "God please help my husband." I will never forget that prayer. By the way baby, Lori, and I came through delivery just fine. She is my treasure.

A picture of the bride in the New Testament emerges, the church of Jesus Christ. She is the bride, the treasure. He is the bridegroom. God uses this image because of its power, passion, intensity, and belonging. Stunning is one of my favorite descriptors.

What embodies the deeper, the richer, that which you wrap your arms when dreams dissolve into despair? I believe that the church of Jesus Christ as expressed in real community is the hope of this planet. I speak with ministers of struggling churches and denominations. I feel heartbroken by the division, the despair, the gridlock of politics and bureaucracy. I listen to post moderns and sense the same angst and anger on the other end of the continuum. Hope exists, but requires surrender and loyalty to unearth. Mega-church strategies are great ideas for megatropolis locations and budgets which can afford the tools and mini-camps, but fail most churches in America. Emergent church ideology is cutting edge, but risks hemorrhaging truth in exchange for meeting the felt needs of post modern believers. There must be another church growth vision which fits the feet of the majority of church communities regardless of denomination or ideology. The hope is Jesus Christ and His treasure, the church. It doesn't begin with mega and post modern, or traditional and obsolete, the vision effects through a transparent heart surrendering to Jesus Christ in real community. The hope can't be music, though important, nor can it be a gifted teacher or leader, though that is good stuff too. The richer reveals healing and help within intimate biblical community. This vision fits the feet and wallet of every missional believer and local church.

May I encourage you? Start small. Pick a pizza joint and a friend. Be brutally truthful about your brokenness. Look to God's word to find the deeper. Share this gift with a few and you will have the richer part of the journey. Take this treasure with you on Sunday mornings. Celebrate the poor preaching and monotone music. Don't exchange your organ pipes for an electric guitar unless all agree or fire your mediocre minister who can't touch the rim. Don't get real big, just get real. Accept everyone and at the same time be loyal to Jesus. Find God's power in your brokenness. Start small but start.

You belong to the greatest truth in human history. May I encourage you to pick the most addicted, abused, nutty person in your congregation and accept. Invite the bikers to your small group, the prostitutes, the perfect people who aren't. Pray for your betrayers and hug them when they quake. Laugh when the wild woman gives you the bird and allow her time to grow. Relax and try not to wrinkle your forehead when converts raise genital questions and rough sex descriptions. They will shock you. When the homosexual shares his pain, let him through the blood-stained doors. Accept without condition, and at the same time be loyal to God without compromise. Grace doesn't happen without loyalty. It is covenant, a mutual embrace. Find a friend and love the depth. Laugh. Be brutally honest about your life and loyal to God and His word. Richness will find you. Delight returns. You will listen again. God will help.

Small Group Bible Study

How sweet is your love, my treasure, my bride! How much better it is than wine . . . You are like a private garden my treasure, my bride! You are like a spring that no one else can drink from, a fountain of my own.
Song of Solomon 4:10-12 NLT

1 .The mystics have enjoyed connecting The Song Of Solomon to a deep love for Jesus. Lori and I have found a secret to an amazing marriage . . . loving Jesus. He is our God and lover of our soul. Look at Ephesians 5 with me.

And further, submit yourselves to one another out of reverence for Christ. For wives this means submit to your husband as you do the Lord . . . For husbands this means love your wives as Christ loved the church. He gave up His life for her . . . .
Ephesians 5.21-25

2. Christian marriage revolves around Jesus. Discuss the role of a wife as it relates to her relationship with Jesus. In the original Greek the text literally says, "Wives be to your husbands as you are to the Lord."

3. Now talk about the role of a husband as he relates to Jesus. Christ was the ultimate servant leader. What does this mean to you and your marriage now, or possible marriage in the future?

Writing Your Story, Healing Your Heart

This is a special story from a friend of mine named Jim. He is one of the fine actors I have ever known, entrepreneur, father, and . . . husband. You will love how he writes and builds his story.

Jim's Story

She didn't have a lick of make up on.

Her hair was a crazy tangle of curls that had been carelessly rammed into a scrunchy, forming a kind of naturally occurring Daniel Boone style coon-skin cap. Her hands gave an appearance of being on the steering wheel of our minivan, but in truth they only floated over the ten and two position because they had to remain nimble for all the other duties (besides steering) they had to perform. Her mouth moved at light speed as she recounted to me all the various activities she was about to engage in the next 48 hours while I was in Minneapolis.

I loved her like this. No make up. Crazy hair. Driving our minivan, so filled with toddler toys that she looked like a mobile Gymboree factory. Merrily rattling off activities as though she was planning the invasion of Normandy. All this while barreling down the 215 to drop me off at MacCarran Airport in Las Vegas.

Becky finished going over her invasion plans and we lapsed into a short silence. I peeked at Olivia, our 3 year old, asleep in her car seat. Even at three, Olivia's large head barely had any hair. The hair that she did have was a translucent fuzz. That big fuzzy head was slumped over as she slept, her lower lip jutting out with the ever present line of drool falling onto her bib.

How I loved this life. I was over come with a deep sense of gratitude, and for a fleeting second my mind drifted.

It hadn't always been like this. Six years before this trip to the airport, I was searching the Bible rigorously looking a loop hole. I was very unhappy. I was unhappy with her. I had been unhappy with her for quite a long time. I was tired of being unhappy so I was looking for a loop hole. The loop hole that I was looking for was something – *anything* – that would allow me to divorce Becky while remaining Scripturally compliant.

Yeah right.

I looked hard. I found nothing. I had been a Christian for over twenty years at that point and I was well aware of the "God hates divorce" drum beat in the church. And I was also aware (although vaguely) of the whole, "the woman needs to serve her husband" deal. I wasn't completely sure what all of that meant, but I was sure that I was getting no service and that had to count for something, I thought.

Way down deep, I knew that no matter how hard I looked, no matter how far I felt Becky fell short in our relationship, no matter how much I thought that my needs weren't being met and the significance of the unhappiness it was causing me, I had no Biblical out. The commitment I made to her on April 23rd, 1988 in a bit of haphazard theatre called a "wedding" was one that I was required to keep. Until death. No take backs.

Well, crap.

At this time, I was 32 years old. The people in my family lived into their eighties. Becky's grandfather was almost 90. If genetics was any indicator of how long she and I would live as husband and wife, it was going to be a long, long, *long* time. I knew that there was no way, that I could simply grit my teeth and face forty five more years in a marriage like this. There was just no way. I couldn't face being this unhappy for that long. Who could, I reasonably asked myself? No one, I concluded. So my search through the Scriptures continued until I found myself in the Gospel of John in the 13th chapter. I had only read this chapter about one million times over the last twenty years.

"Jesus washed the disciples' feet, blah, blah, blah."

Jesus, the Son of God, was on His knees washing a particularly unclean piece of the human body and then standing up and saying that this was His example to us that we should follow. Pretty straight forward stuff, I had always thought. I'd even been through those fairly awkward ceremonies in small groups where we'd wash each other's feet and then say afterward how "moving" it was. It was never moving for me. It was always odd. For me, it was just another bit of empty (although well meaning) theatre.

And then it happened.

God spoke to me–clear, even. Unmistakable.

"Jim, wash her feet."

Everything seemed to stop. I sat, frozen, at my desk in the dining room of my little apartment in West Hollywood. I vaguely heard street sounds wafting through an open window, but everything within a 3 foot radius from where I was sitting was absolutely still.

The concept of what I had just heard was permeating my skin. It was oozing into my muscles. It was dripping into my bones. It was gently, powerfully, irreversibly penetrating my DNA.

"Wash her feet."

"Wash Becky's feet."

I quietly closed my Bible and began to think.

I immediately started compiling a mental list of what serving Becky would look like. I decided that I would never mention her weight again. I would never push having sex on her again. I would never compare her, verbally, with anyone ever again. I would take seriously everything - *everything* - she said to me and act on it. If she asked me to do something, I would do it. If she asked me not to do something, I would stop. I would work to listen to her without mentally or emotionally attempting to maneuver her to adopt my personal agenda. I would try to understand what *she* wanted and give it to her without comment or complaint. I would examine all of my behavior and evaluate it against how it would make her feel. I would modify all of my behavior so that, to the greatest extent possible, I would eliminate anything that caused her pain, embarrassment, sadness or anger. And, most importantly, as I did these things in increasing measure, I would expect no reward from her. My mission to do them was simply because it was Jesus' example and command.

Now, make no mistake–I did have a hope of a reward in all of this. The reward that I was hoping for was, somehow, someway to find joy in marriage and in life. I would go so far as to say that I would have had no hope of long term success in this mission if somehow joy didn't emerge out of what I was doing. But I had a vague sense, very early on, that the joy I was looking for wasn't ultimately going to be conveyed to me by receiving effusive "thank-yous" from my wife because of all of my so-called "big changes." What I was looking for, without really understanding it at the time, was something even bigger than that. Deeper. I was seeking treasure.

I made no announcement to Becky that I begun this mission. I didn't want to taint what I was doing by saying anything. As I considered my new way of thinking, I began to realize what a jerk I had been for most our marriage. I began to realize that, really, the only person I actually cared about in this relationship was me. I was realizing that everything–quite literally *everything*–in our relationship was done ultimately for my benefit and by my design. I specified what we were going to do and I evaluated the results of what we did by criteria that I developed with no input from anyone. And–surprise, surprise–I always measured up very well and Becky rarely measured up at all.

And so, I began my attempt. I began my attempt to wash Becky's feet. I began my attempt to serve her without reservation or condition.

What happened next is difficult to describe. As I committed more and more to washing her feet, slowly over time, I began to witness, quite literally, a transformation. The interesting thing about transformations is you can never be too sure who it is that is actually being transformed. Each legitimate act of service on my part seemed to unlock something within her. I started to become aware that there was another woman entering my life. The qualities that this woman possessed were alluring. She had an ease that my wife didn't have. This woman smiled a lot. She was so open. I was aware of how sensitive she was. The smallest thing could make her sad or happy. More and more I found myself hating the idea of her being sad and it became fuel to me in my pursuit to serve her. Each smile was a victory, each frown required a mental note to do better in the future.

But then it got weird.

She seemed to develop a rather strong interest in me. She wanted to know what I thought of things. But this woman didn't push, or poke or shame me into a ridiculous, (and usually grotesquely self-serving) linguistic act that Christian's commonly call, "sharing." She just wanted to talk with me. And her ease as she approached me to talk was irresistible.

I talked to her. She listened to what I said. She talked to me. And with every fiber of my being, I listened. Unexplainably, I was overcome with a *need* to listen. It was primal. To not listen would be a violation of her trust and, at this point, that was unthinkable. I knew I was on very dangerous ground now. How had I let this get so out of hand? I could see what was happening. I was forging a very deep, very thick emotional bond with this woman. I was in love with her.

What would I tell my wife?

But this woman was my wife. She had always been my wife. I just never knew it. I could never see it. Up until this moment, I wasn't the man she needed so that she could reveal her true self. But here she was now. It was sweet. We experienced joy. And then a whirlwind of events exploded into fast forward: We got pregnant, my job started going great, our baby daughter was born, we bought our first home in Southern California, bought our first brand new minivan, my job got even better, Becky stayed home full time, we had a great church, our relationship deepened, my job moved us to Las Vegas, we bought our dream home, we found a great church in Vegas, our relationship deepened, we began to try for our second child, I started my own business, we sold our dream home and bought our forever home, we made great friends at church and our relationship deepened. And deepened.

We continued to barrel down the 215 toward the airport and a faint smile crept across my face. I was on my way to a meeting to hopefully strike the first deal in my new business. And this was going to be a big one. My little firm (consisting of my partner, me and our attorney) was going to bring a well established regional airline, based in Minneapolis, together with an innovative vacation company to create low-cost, high end vacation packages for travelers who lived in the Midwest. My company would earn a commission on every vacation sold. This was an important meeting. There was a lot of money on the table and both the CEO of the airline and the President of the vacation company would be in the room with me. Becky would spend her time while I was away for the next few days unpacking the boxes that littered our new home and would finish painting the kitchen and family room. My smile broadened slightly when I thought of the last two weeks as Becky agonized over what color to paint the walls. Paint was everywhere. This was our forever home and the color had to be perfect. So, there were swatches of color splashed on walls all over the house. She wanted to see what the colors looked like in the morning, in the evening, at sunrise and sunset. I didn't really have a preference for the color. But I knew that this was important to her, so I gave her the space she needed to go through this process, knowing that when she discovered the perfect color, it would make her very happy. And, of course, she discovered the color and she was ecstatic.

We pulled into the departing passengers lane at MacCarren airport and it was as I expected, a chaotic knot of cars, buses, taxis, people and luggage all struggling in every direction. Becky navigated our Chrysler Town and County to the Southwest terminal. Olivia was still asleep as I jumped out of the van and pulled my suitcase out of the back. I was going to poke my head back through the passenger side window to tell Becky goodbye and that I loved her, when I realized that she had gotten out of the van and was standing right next to me.

She had that look.

This was a look that I had come to know very well over the last few years. This was the, "I need a kiss, please" look. I quickly obliged by giving her a short peck on the lips then quickly turned away to grab my suitcase. There was a lot of traffic and I knew the airport cops were going to be on us in another second if Becky didn't get our car moving. As I picked up my suitcase, I felt a firm grasp on my arm. I turned around to see my wife standing there holding me firm, looking directly at me. She took her free arm and slid it around my neck, pulling me to her.

And she kissed me.

One of the things I knew about my wife was that she did not like public displays of affection. That was one of her "things." Hand holding was ok, but kissing beyond the simple peck on the lips was strictly off limits. So it was mildly surprising when she went to the trouble of getting out of the van for a kiss in such a public place. I gave her the kind of kiss I thought she expected—sincere, but short and fast. But on this day, in this chaotic gridlock of people, luggage and exhaust she gave me the kind of kiss that was reserved for when we were alone. It was the kind of kiss makes a man not want to get on an airplane.

She stepped back from me smiling at the shock on my face. "Call me when you get there," she said.

The next time I saw my wife was in the intensive care unit of University Medical Center in Las Vegas. Less than 24 hours from the time I kissed her goodbye, she was hit by a pick-up truck running a red light at a busy intersection on the 215. I had rushed back from Minneapolis when I received the call that she had been in a car accident. But, the full understanding of the size and severity of what I was facing didn't hit me until I stood in that hospital room looking at her. Half of her head was shaved clean. Gleaming in the antiseptic glare of the room's light were the 40 metal stitches that held together the left side of her ghoulishly swollen head. The hair that remained on her head was soaked in blood. Her left eye had been pushed from it's socket past the bridge of her nose. A tube was in her mouth held in place by tangle of surgical tape. Blood and puss oozed from her ears and nose. Her entire body was buried under a mountain of tubes and wires. Her chest rose and fell with mechanical precision and in perfect time to a sucking sound made by the machine, the size of a refrigerator, at the side of her bed. My eyes drifted slowly over her and she was all but unrecognizable to me in that moment.

And then I saw her feet. They were uncovered. They had no blood on them. There were no tubes running in or out of them. They were slightly pink. I recognized them immediately. They were my wife's feet. I reached out to touch them and they were cold. Becky hated having cold feet. She was always wearing socks. I rubbed my hands together and pressed them to her left foot and then her right, repeating this process until I could feel her skin starting to warm.

As I stood there, I began to consider how she and I would get through this. But deep down, I knew. Nothing had changed. God had spoken to me on this subject almost 5 years before.

"Jim, wash her feet."

And, by God's grace, that is what I endeavored to do, even to this day.

Write Your Story

If you are married or divorced write your marriage story. Can you blend in the story of your parents, your brokenness and that of your spouse or ex spouse? Can you identify your attachments or idols which have undermined your marriage? If you are single, can you reflect on your brokenness as a single person and how this may impact your future marriage? What is the treasure of your marriage or singleness? Can you identify with Jim's addiction to happiness?

Write Your Story

Conclusion

A POST MODERN mother of three small children sits on a bench outside a hospital waiting for a ride. She slouches slightly soothing awkward pregnancy physics. A beautiful Dutch woman takes a seat nearby. She admires the three children and notices the mother beginning to labor. The Dutch woman enters the adjacent medical building seeking help. Three times with increasing urgency she enters the hospital greeted by blank stares and indecision. No response. It is as though the hospital staff cannot listen. Perhaps liability concerns, litigation. The point becomes crystal clear, no one helps the excruciating ordeal of the mom.

On the third trip back from the hospital the Dutch woman finds the mother on her back, the head of the baby visibly pressing through maternity pants. Like an action hero, the Dutch woman strips off the mother's clothing in front of God and three pairs of wide little eyes. The silent infant lay motionless; the mother's undergarments strangling. The Dutch woman frees the newborn, resuscitates tiny lungs until an exquisite cacophony pierces the panic. With sensitive slender hands she soothes the child, amniotic fluid glistens in warm rays of sun, innocent eyes search for love and belonging, fingers grasp, miniature legs run in mid air. The infant lives.

As she holds the newborn, a physician arrives. He multi tasks analyzing while at the same time installing latex gloves. He then cuts the cord, and wraps the infant. The physician receives acclaim for great courage. His name appears in the paper. Regional news media herald him for heroism. Little does the world know that neither physician, latex, nor lateness saved the child.

The Dutch woman is the hero . . . my wife. Lori saved the child. Though the local newspaper and witnesses knew the truth, the story stood without correction.

The glove wearing physician owes the Dutch woman flowers. Had it not been for her, the child was DOA. There would be neither accolades nor newspaper herald for delivering a dead baby. A litigious society seeks scapegoats. Someone would pay.

In a stale visceral stall, a third world teen mom birthed the light of the world. Jesus Christ emerged in a crummy neighborhood, dungeon-like, with the glamour of a meat locker. I visited the historic location of His birth in Bethlehem, horrible, dark, subterranean. But here the treasure uncovered where blue-collar shepherds and wide eyed eastern astrologers watched in amazement. In an underground feed trough God brought to light the greatest gift in human history.

Jesus is our great treasure. Born in the horrendous, depressing, and hidden, he now kneels in that same place with tender hands and brings us to birth. He holds the broken hearted with nail-scarred hands, glistening in love's light and grace. Christ becomes the scapegoat for listening meltdown. Attachments drive through His divinity like Roman nails. Low velocity blood spatter covers shame. Pierced feet bear the appalling burden of abuse. There is nothing sanitary about the cross, only purity, passion, and the resurrection of Jesus Christ.

Church growth ideologies and superficial spirituality can cover truth like a latex glove. Sanitary, but not *sanctus*. I stand with my ministry buddies and talk about touching the rim. Each pastor from mainline denominations I know tells a personal story of addiction, trauma, or abuse in his or her life. Look at our collective modern history in America. A leader of a mega church and a nation of evangelicals resigns because of indiscretions with a gay masseur and confessions of illegal drug transactions. We all have a story. The church in the 'hood stands as a metaphor for every reader. You have a story. In late night ceiling staring sessions with God brokenness emerges seeking wholeness. With an overcoat of grace and tenderness Christ covers shame. With gentle hands the father embraces. He will not be late or cover up the richness of His grace. Jesus Christ, our physician and healer, cannot lie or squander your pain.

Still can't slam-dunk? Shoot the ball where you can score from. What if the local church or denomination you are in is exactly where a sovereign loving-God wants you? Your faith community, family, marriage, singleness bleed, you see weaknesses . . . good. Lean close to His power. Post modern ideological analysis can lead to paralyzing anger. May I encourage you toward the pursuit of treasure? Shoot with passionate tenderness not rage.

I believe the next great awakening of spirituality in America will happen in hundreds of thousands of intimate communities of believers. Imagine these transparent whole Christians in small groups gathering during the week. Then, on Sundays they recalibrate and re-celebrate with liturgy, music, transformational offerings, and spiritually deep tradition remembering the goodness of God.

What if that movement of God's Spirit is taking place now?

So friend, tuck in your franchise jersey and tighten your Hawaiian flowered shorts. Lace up your Air-Galileans and cynical sensitivities. Take a victory lap around the arena . . . you are His treasure! For all the short folk with small feet who can't dunk, but who passionately love leading others to the rim . . . shoot.

Small Group Bible Study

God Almighty will be your treasure, more wealth than you can imagine. You'll take delight in God, the Mighty one, and look to Him joyfully, boldly. You'll pray to Him and He'll listen; He'll help you do what you've promised.
Job 22:25 MSG

I love this passage coming from Eliphaz, a man who did not have his act completely together. What I see in the Treasure passages is a deep life with Jesus in simple bite sized pieces. The Holy Spirit has inspired an amazing spirituality which focuses on the person of God and Jesus. Look at this passage in several translations.

1. What is our treasure, the greatest good, the goal of our life?

2. What are the results?

3. What kind of connection do we have with Him? Where can we find help?

4. How is this different than spiritual ideas or movements you have been a part of? Can you have a conversation about the beauty and simplicity of the Treasure?

Writing Your Story, Healing Your Heart

Now, begin to rewrite your story. Instead of you as the main character place Jesus as the central figure. He stands at each disappointment and touches every broken place. Your weaknesses now become His strength. The perpetrators find forgiveness. You stand forgiven. You are whole. In your story show how your brokenness which is now the power of God in your life touches others. The gift continues.

This is our last gathering. Bring Kleenex. Receive communion and be thankful for what God has done for you. Thank Him for treasure. Check out Clare's story below. Reflect how the broken places have become her strength. Talk about how you can be in another group together. Invite an unchurched friend who needs help and healing. Keep the revolution moving friend! Healing communities believe in sharing this gift with others. You must not keep it to yourself. The book you hold in your hands now contains a very special story of healing and help. I wonder what creative ways you can share your story with others? I would love to hear your ideas, feel free to blog me at glenmaiden.com.

Clare's Story

I am in a place right now where I see God as my father, my mother, my husband . . . each of these roles perfectly performed for me, by my God.

Biological mothers and fathers that raise us physically are just human with flaws. But they are human, and they are God's children also. I choose to see them now in this light.

The love and example and encouragement that I craved from my parents . . . . I find in God now. This allows me to free my biological parents from this role. The acceptance, love, cherishing, encouragement, that I desire as a wife, I have in God . . . because I am God's bride . . . he does not blame me, does not try to diagnose me, does not attack me, or hurt me. He is the perfect relationship for me . . . mother, father, husband, God . . . . I look to Him, and he helps me maintain my emotional stability in the hurricane that is my life. I am mending my relationships. There is much progress and hope . . . through Jesus.

Today I have hope through prayer. I am just thankful that I have been able to heal as much as I have so far to see God as my REAL father releases my parents of all the expectations I had for them. It's so nice. I am no longer afraid of being abandoned, because I KNOW that God will never abandon me, he will ALWAYS take care of me. There is such peace in that knowledge!

I know God will not suffocate me and guilt trip me and threaten me . . . I am safe as long as I turn to Him . . . Trust Him, love Him, have faith in Him.

Write Your Story

Write Your Story